finding the law
becring 5th ed

SUCCESSFUL LEGAL ANALYSIS AND WRITING:

THE FUNDAMENTALS

Second Edition

Bradley G. Clary
Clinical Professor and
Director of Applied Legal Instruction
University of Minnesota Law School

Pamela Lysaght
Associate Professor of Law and
Director of Applied Legal Theory and Analysis
University of Detroit Mercy School of Law

THOMSON
WEST

Mat #40479757

© West, a Thomson business, 2003
© 2006 Thomson/West
    610 Opperman Drive
    P.O. Box 64526
    St. Paul, MN 55164–0526
    1–800–328–9352

Printed in the United States of America

ISBN–13: 978–0–314–16915–0
ISBN–10: 0–314–16915–6

 TEXT IS PRINTED ON 10% POST CONSUMER RECYCLED PAPER

DEDICATIONS

To all of the hard working legal writing teachers
who labor every day to help law students become
accomplished lawyers.

B.G.C.
P.L.

To Mary-Louise—for being there.
B.G.C.

To Leon—for eternity.
P.L.

ACKNOWLEDGEMENTS

We are indebted to many persons who have helped us along the way in our careers and in the preparation of this book.

We thank Douglas Powell and Pamela Siege Chandler, who had the confidence in us to encourage the publication of this text. We also thank Pam and her colleague Heidi Hellekson for their review of early drafts and their helpful comments and suggestions.

We thank Katherine Donohue for all her dedication and hard work in assisting us with this text; Bethany Tkach Abrams, Maya Parekh, Emily Pruisner, and Kevin Toll for their help in researching and cite-checking; Susan Miller for her assistance in formatting portions of the work, as well as helping us keep our senses of humor; and Barbara White for her assistance in coordinating the copying and shipping of drafts of this text.

We acknowledge the work of legal writing student instructors Deborah Behles, Rachel Brass, Oliver Kim, and Tara Tilbury in assisting in the original research in the spring of 2000 into the law of the First Circuit and others in the Commonwealth Hospital problem that appears in Chapter 12. A version of this problem was initially conceived in a slightly different form by Author Clary and Professor Susanna Sherry in connection with the work of legal writing sections attached to Professor Sherry's civil procedure class that spring.

We thank Ryan Kelly, John Hutchinson, Maya Parekh, and Joshua Heggem for their help over the years in researching and drafting variations on the Chris Smith problem found in the Teacher's Manual to this text.

We thank several students, as well as some colleagues, for their assistance with developing various case files included in the Teacher's Manual: For the *U.S. v. Nelson* problem, Bethany Tkach Abrams and Jeffrey Paulsen; for the *U.S. v. Harper* problem, Adam Trampe and Joshua Heggem; and for the *U.S. v. Martins* problem, Kevin Toll, John Kelly, and Professor Weissman.

Brad Clary thanks former and current student teaching partners Deborah Behles, David Schelzel, Dawn Kim, Jennifer Rogers, Anna Dunbar-

Hester, and Nicola Kieves for their help in teaching the small section classes that helped inform his ideas for this book.

Pamela Lysaght thanks her colleagues, Cristina Lockwood, Danielle Istl, Cara Cunningham, Deborah Paruch, Michelle Streicher, Tracy Weissman, and Pamela Wilkins for their invaluable insights and support. And she thanks her students who helped inspire many of the ideas in presenting the material for this book.

Finally, Brad and Pam wish to thank Mary-Louise, Ben, Sam, and Leon for their much-appreciated and invaluable support, patience, and grace during the drafting process.

TABLE OF CONTENTS

PREFACE i

CHAPTER 1
Road Mapping 1
    Where, What 2
    Why 2
    Who 2
    When 3
    How 3
    Example 4
    Comparison to Legal Writing 7
    Conclusion 10

CHAPTER 2
The Role of Facts in Resolving Legal Problems 11
    Story Identification 12
    Additional Story Identification Principles 16
    Conclusion 17

CHAPTER 3
The Role of Rules in Resolving Legal Problems 19
    The Sources of Rules: Enacted Law and Cases 19
        1.   Enacted Law 20
        2.   Cases 23
    Basic Principles for Understanding Primary Authority 25
    Considerations When Working with Statutes and Cases ... 28

CHAPTER 4
Determining the Rule in Typical, Simple Scenarios 31
    Pulling Apart a Rule 31
    Common Mistakes in Parsing a Rule 36
    Assembling a Rule from a Single Court Decision 38

CHAPTER 5
Determining the Rule in Typical, Complex Scenarios 49
    Assembling a Rule from Multiple Court Decisions 49
    Common Mistakes in Assembling a Rule
        from Multiple Cases 61

CHAPTER 6
Determining the Rule in Atypical Scenarios 63
    Assembling Rules in Atypical Settings: Direct Conflicts 63
    Assembling Rules in Atypical Settings:
        Cases of First Impression 67
    Conclusion 71

CHAPTER 7
Determining the Meaning of a Statutory Rule 73
    Interpreting Statutory Language..73
    Conclusion 81

CHAPTER 8
Basic Organizing Principles in Legal Analysis and Writing 83
    IRAC: The Basic Components 86
        1.   Introduction 86
        2.   Rule 88
        3.   Application 91
        4.   Conclusion 93
    Linking Discrete IRACs 94
    Conclusion 98

CHAPTER 9
Basic Writing Principles 99
    Prefer Simplicity 100
    Prefer the Familiar 101
    Prefer Concision 101
    Prefer Action 101
    Avoid Overuse of Adjectives and Adverbs 102
    Pay Attention to Flow 102

Be Meticulous 103
Common Mistakes to Avoid... 103

CHAPTER 10
Citation and Quotation Basics 105
ALWD Citation Manual 107
  General Citation Rules 107
    Full and Short Citations 108
    Pinpoint References 108
    Citation Placement and Use 108
    Abbreviations 109
    Capitalization 112
  Citing to Primary Authority 112
    Constitutions currently in force 112
    Statutes currently in force 112
    Cases 115
  Citing to Secondary Authority 117
    Restatements 117
    Legal Periodicals (Law Reviews)........................... 118
    Books 119
  Working with Signals 120
The Bluebook 122
  General Citation Rules 122
    Full and Short Citations 122
    Pinpoint References 123
    Citation Placement and Use 123
    Abbreviations 124
    Capitalization 127
  Citing to Primary Authority 127
    Constitutions currently in force 127
    Statutes currently in force 128
    Cases 130
  Citing to Secondary Authority 132
    Restatements 132
    Legal Periodicals (Law Reviews) 133
    Books 134
  Working with Signals 135
  General Rules on Quoting Authority 137
    Block Quotations 137

Shorter Quotations 138
Alterations and Omissions 138
Common Questions about When and What to Cite 141

CHAPTER 11
Communicating a Predictive Analysis 145
Common Features of Good Predictive Writing 146
The Office Memorandum Template 153
The Client Advice Letter Template 161

CHAPTER 12
Communicating a Persuasive Analysis 169
Common Features of Good Persuasive Writing 170
The Trial Court Brief Template 175
The Appellate Brief Template 202

PREFACE

This is a book about legal analysis and writing for first-year law students. There are many fine books about these topics on the market. A reader might well ask—why one more? We set out in this preface our fundamental design premise, our fundamental theme, six principles that beginning legal writers need to understand, and features inherent in good legal analysis and communication.

The Fundamental Design Premise:
Flexible Components and Templates

In our experience, many of the texts currently on the market are comprehensive; that is, they tend to be designed for an entire course—a form of one-stop shopping. They offer considerable advice on many aspects of analysis and writing. They are very good, but precisely because of their length and comprehensiveness, they are not always ready-references. Further, they may offer advice that is either beyond a given law school's legal writing program goals or that has to be affirmatively explained away as at least partially inconsistent with that professor's different advice. (This may be inescapable for any text on legal analysis and writing. Our goal is to minimize significantly this potential problem.) Comprehensive texts are not necessarily what every purchaser wants.

A possible analogy is to stereo equipment: Some purchasers want to buy a completely integrated unit. The turntable, the disc player, the speakers, the receiver and other equipment are all pre-assembled in a single product. There is no design work for the purchaser to do. No assembly is required. All the bells and whistles are included. There is one convenient package. But it is, of course, the manufacturer's package.

Some purchasers, on the other hand, want to build the stereo system to fit their own particular needs. They want a particular type of speaker. They want a different disc player. They want basic functionality, and then they want to add their own bells and whistles. The integrated package from the manufacturer provides great value, but not the flexibility they want. Instead, they want only certain basic components, to which they will make their own additions.

Our book adopts a basic component approach to legal writing. Legal writers can assemble a competent analysis and written product by mastering the concepts in this book. They can also mix and match the pieces they want. Additional bells and whistles are for individual professors and students to add, to fit the programs at their own law schools.

The Fundamental Theme: Problem Solving

We think there is a place for a book on legal analysis and writing that expressly looks at those subjects through a problem-solving lens. Consider one of the cases in a first-year doctrinal text in contracts, torts, or criminal law. Does it just drop into place? No, someone's life story was rolling along. A problem developed. "The law" stepped in to solve the problem through the efforts of lawyers and other persons. Those efforts followed a standard sequence: The lawyers first had to learn the facts of the story and identify the problem. Then the lawyers had to identify the potentially applicable legal principles and analyze them. Once the lawyers analyzed the principles, the lawyers had to apply them to the facts of the problem. That analysis reached a conclusion as to how "the law" does and/or should resolve the problem. The lawyers then communicated the analysis to one or more audiences—a client, a colleague, a judge, an adversary, or others. In the end, a court picked a resolution among competing choices as to the facts, the law, or both, and the authors of the casebook elected to publish the court's decision to illustrate a legal proposition. This selection occurred far down the line. The lawyers did considerable work long before the court decided the case, and long before the casebook authors decided to include the case in their texts.

This book is about the work of lawyers. We provide fundamental advice and templates for analyzing and discussing legal problems from the standpoint of practicing lawyers who have to help solve them. For this purpose, we think of lawyers as being on a two-stage expedition, which we will reflect in the organization of the balance of this book. The first stage is to assemble the material required for a successful expedition to solve a problem. At this stage, we focus upon a standard road-mapping sequence of identifying the problem with specificity, identifying the key facts in the relevant story that give rise to the problem, identifying with specificity the legal rules that might potentially apply to the problem, analyzing the relevant legal rules and applying them to the material facts, and identifying a solution to the relevant problem. The second stage, once the lawyers have assembled all of the key material, is to communicate the expedition's route to anyone who has to move with the expedition to the proposed solution. At this stage, we focus upon the creation of such types of legal documents as office memoranda, client letters, trial court briefs, and appellate court briefs.

SIX KEY PRINCIPLES

1. Legal analysis and writing are audience-focused.

Because legal analysis and writing are fundamentally about problem solving, they must be audience-focused. The logic is simple: The relevant story is not the lawyer's story. The relevant problem is not the lawyer's problem. The legal principles are not the lawyer's principles. The ultimate decision-maker is not the lawyer. Instead, the story is the client's. The problem is the client's. The legal principles are the court's or the legislature's. The ultimate decision-makers are the juries and judges (in litigated cases), or the clients (in settled cases and in transactions that do not result in litigation), or other persons or entities such as agencies, colleagues, and adversaries (in various settings). These are all audiences.

As a result, the writer has to evaluate constantly how his or her analysis and communication will be received by others. And audiences these days often share some of the following characteristics: They are busy. They have too much to do and too little time in which to do it. They are on information overload. They are used to getting information in sound bites. They want quick answers. They want solutions. They want efficiency. They want to simplify their lives.

We assume that our audience shares some of these characteristics. Thus, we aim to be short. We aim to be efficient. We aim to simplify.

2. Legal writing is hard work.

Problem solving is not easy. Communicating solutions so that an audience will both understand and adopt the solutions is not easy. This is all true—even with standard sequences and templates—and frustrating.

Picture a typical law student—bright, eager, academic achiever, maybe an English major, in law school to learn "the law." Consider that typical law student's potential reaction to a required first-year legal writing course: "I already know how to write. I don't need college entry-level English again." Concede also for present purposes that the reaction is accurate as far as it goes.

Even so, the immediate reaction is not on the mark. First-year legal writing courses are not a repeat of college freshman English. They are instead fundamentally courses about what it means to be a lawyer. And they are not just courses about "writing." They are instead courses about how to piece together a story, how to identify problems, how to think about "the law," how to parse legal rules, how to analyze and apply legal principles, how to determine what legal conclusion will solve a given problem, and how to reach a legal audience in writing. Lawyers spend their entire careers perfecting these skills. There are a lot of moving pieces that have to come together. This book aims to help law students understand those, through hard work.

3. Legal analysis and writing are learn-by-doing tasks.

For the most part, the only way to get good at analyzing and writing about solutions to legal problems is to practice. So what beginning legal writers need the most are a series of steps to follow and a set of simple templates that serve as models. Hard work and feedback are key ingredients to developing these skills.

Thus, this book is about basic building blocks and the sequence for using them. Beyond the basics, however, the book is short on additional commentary. We do not intend to be comprehensive. Readers tend not to absorb detailed nuances that may arise in thousands of different configurations unless they can place those nuances in the context of their own specific projects. We count on professors to practice students on the details they think their students most need to know to fit their own course designs.

4. Legal analysis and writing require the ability to multi-task.

A good piece of legal writing involves the integration of many tasks—assembling and disassembling facts, assembling and disassembling rules, re-looking at facts, re-looking at rules, applying rules to facts, reaching conclusions, and communicating conclusions. We are going to set out a sequence for these tasks, essentially in the order of the chapters in this text. But do not be misled by the linear sequence of the chapters. In practice, a lawyer will be engaged in many of the tasks more or less simultaneously, moving back and forth among them.

5. *Legal analysis and writing require living with ambiguity.*

Legal rules are living things. They expand. They change. They contract. They find new application. They, like life generally, are often ambiguous. Even though there may be standard concepts that most persons can accept, reasonable people may differ over what "the law" says, what it should say, and how it should apply to a specific given problem.[1]

The same can be said of the process of legal analysis and communication. Some templates tend to be more effective than others. Some methodologies tend to be more effective than others. We intend to set out in this book some approaches we think are generally acceptable to help you present consistently competent work product to your audiences. But reasonable legal writing teachers may prefer different advice in a given circumstance. None of them may be affirmatively "wrong;" each is making a different judgment about the best of alternative acceptable choices. This is an important point with which beginning legal writers must become comfortable. The key is to be able to explain why one judgment is preferred over another.

6. *Legal analysis and writing are messy, but the final work product cannot be.*

The process of thinking about solutions to legal problems and the process for producing an initial draft of a legal writing are messy. There are starts and stops. There are circles and semi-circles. There are reversals of direction. There are detours and unintended wrong turns. It is not uncommon for a lawyer to think she is dealing with one set of facts, research the law, begin applying the law, and discover that there are new or additional facts. It is not uncommon for a lawyer to think that one set of legal principles is relevant, only to find a lead to a new legal argument that heads in a different direction. It is not uncommon for a lawyer to arrive tentatively at one solution

---

[1] If everyone agreed on the rule or rules for any given circumstance in life, society would not need lawyers. Everyone would just consult the rulebook and cut out the middleman.

to a problem, only to talk herself out of that first solution and into a different second one, in drafting the memorandum explaining the first.

Beginning legal writers need to understand that all of this is natural. Starting and stopping, thinking and re-thinking, writing and re-writing are all parts of the relevant process. Just make sure, to the extent practical, that there is enough time set aside for the project to allow the full process to play out. Also, just remember that the final written work product the audience sees should not be a stream-of-consciousness recitation of the messy analytical and drafting process. Rather, the final written work product the audience sees must be clean, simple, straightforward, logical, and flow irresistibly to a solution to the legal problem at hand.

FEATURES OF GOOD ANALYSIS AND WRITING

What are the features, then, of a competent process and a competent final work product? Below are simple ones to keep in mind, no matter what type of legal analysis or communication you may be generating.

First, think.

It is hard to make a point if you have not developed a point to make. Ask yourself:

> ➢ What is the story I am analyzing?
> ➢ What is the problem?
> ➢ What are the potentially relevant legal rules?
> ➢ How do they apply to the problem?
> ➢ What is my solution to the problem?
> ➢ How can I best convey that to a reader?

Then, make your point.

Accurately. Accuracy involves honest fact statements, accurate citations to sources, and precision in details.

Clearly. Clarity involves eliminating ambiguity; preferring specifics to generalities; using road maps; and following a logical, organized structure.

Concisely. Concision involves eliminating excess language, getting to the point, and separating the relevant from the irrelevant.

Responsibly. Responsibility involves a sense of ownership of the process and product, a sense of fair play, a sense of professionalism, and avoiding inappropriate language and name-calling,

In your own way. As a writer, you still have to "be yourself." Otherwise, you are not credible. Incorporate within your own personal style the various processes and templates that will help you best make your point.

Work and rework. Edit and re-edit.

The reader of a typical piece of legal writing has to be able to understand the writer's point, see how to get there, and (especially in the case of persuasive writing) want to get there with the writer.

Editing is not just about checking details of work such as spelling, punctuation, sentence structure, and citation form, although such checking is vital. Editing is also about making sure that you have made a point your reader understands, can get to, and wants to get to.

Critique your work.

Unless you run out of time, do not stop working on your analysis and writing until you are satisfied with your answers to these questions:

➢ Do I understand the relevant story?

➢ Do I understand the problem to solve?

➢ Do I understand the legal principles that might apply?

➢ Have I analyzed and applied those principles to the facts?

➢ Have I reached a conclusion that will solve the problem from my client's standpoint?

➢ Does my writing make the relevant point(s) to my reader?

➢ Will the reader understand?

➢ Will the reader follow?

➢ Will the reader accept?

As these questions demonstrate, the final stages of critiquing require the writer to shift focus—from the writer's perspective to the reader's perspective. In other words, effective self-critique requires evaluating your work product through the lens of the intended audience.

The focus of the rest of this book is on how to use these principles and features to successfully solve legal problems and communicate the analysis to your intended audience.

CHAPTER 1

Road Mapping

The process of communicating a legal analysis can be thought of as a form of road mapping. The lawyer is taking a visitor (the audience) to a destination (the solution to a legal problem). When a legal writer is preparing an office memorandum, a client letter, a trial court brief, an appellate brief, or a transactional document such as a contract, the writer should be thinking in terms of giving directions. To give good directions, a lawyer should think in terms of a standard where, what, why, who, when, and how template. Then the lawyer should apply that template in giving directions.[1]

---

[1] Two other forms of this concept have previously appeared in Bradley G. Clary, Sharon Reich Paulsen, & Michael J. Vanselow, *Advocacy on Appeal* 2d ed. 18-20 (West 2004); Bradley G. Clary & Deborah N. Behles, *Roadmapping and Legal Writing*, 8 Persp. 134-36 (2000); *see also* Kathy L. Cerminara, *Metaphors Help Students Write More Logically*, L. Teacher 2 (Spring 1997); Brian S. Williams, *Road Maps, Tour Guides, and Parking Lots: The Use of Context in Teaching Overview and Thesis Paragraphs*, 7 Persp. 27 (1998). Those of you who may be journalists will recognize the who, what, where, when, why, and how questions from your training in that field. *E.g.* Kristie Bunton et al., *Writing Across the Media* 105 (Bedford/St. Martin's 1999).

Where, What

Where do you want to take the visitor? *What* are your goals? *What* do you want the visitor to do upon arrival at the destination? We combine the where and what questions for present purposes, because they are so closely related in this setting. Those are the first questions you have to ask. To answer them, your analysis of the relevant legal problem, and your proposed solution, must be clear in your mind. You cannot send a visitor to a destination if you do not know what that is or what you want your visitor to do there. So spend the necessary time to figure out those questions.[2]

Why

Why do you want to take the visitor to *that* destination? Presumably you believe that the destination you have chosen (the proposed solution to the relevant legal problem) is desirable. What good will come from the result? Will the visitor (audience) benefit? If so, how? In the legal context, will the client benefit? If so, how? Will society benefit? If so, how? Will third parties benefit? If so, how?

Who

Who is your visitor (audience)? For example, does your visitor have any prior knowledge of the destination (is your client/the judge/a colleague already familiar with the kinds of legal analyses and solutions that are appropriate in the present matter)? Does the visitor need intricately detailed directions, or just a reminder of the general route (are there already letters/memoranda/briefs in the matter with which the audience is familiar)? And does your visitor follow directions best when there are visual aids (a picture map); when there are numbered steps (first, proceed left out of the

---

[2] Note that you may not fully develop your analysis and proposed solution of a problem until you actually write it out. That is fine. Your first draft of a road map does not have to be, indeed probably should not be, the draft you actually give your visitor. You may change your mind on the proper destination or the route to get there. Leave yourself enough time to revise the written work product so that it reflects the final version of your analysis and solution, as opposed to the messy interim work.

parking lot to the second traffic light; second, turn right at the light; third, proceed to . . . .); when there are landmarks (turn left at the traffic light where you see the ABC Supermarket on the corner); or a combination of these? In other words, what kind of a learner is your audience?[3] *Be aware of your audience*

When

When are you leading your visitor to the destination? Are you going there now (you have a problem whose solution depends upon the law and the facts that currently exist)? Or are you going there in the future (you have a problem whose solution depends upon your prediction as to the law and the facts that will likely exist at some future relevant time)?

How

How are you leading your visitor to the destination? There are a variety of possibilities:

➢ Are you sending the visitor by a scenic route, or the most direct one?

➢ Are you sending the visitor by a leisurely route, or the fastest one?

➢ Are you sending the visitor by the safest route, or a riskier one?

➢ Are you sending the visitor by the most familiar route, or a newer one?

➢ Are you sending the visitor by the easiest route, or a more difficult one?

---

[3] Have you and a partner ever attempted to assemble a toy, a piece of furniture, a stereo, or something similar? Some persons need to take out the manufacturer's manual, read all of the directions step-by-step, and then look at the picture of the finished product before commencing any actual assembly. Other persons can simply dump the contents of the box on the floor, look at the components, and go to work. Both will wind up in the end with the same product, but each will have approached assembly in a very different way. Similarly, legal audiences will have different learning styles that need to be recognized and accommodated.

> ➤ Are you sending the visitor by the currently fashionable route, or a more traditional one?

There may not be one single correct answer. The choices likely depend upon the answers to the previous where, what, why, who, and when questions. For example, in a legal writing setting, your visitor (audience) will often be a busy person. So you do not want a leisurely road map to the relevant problem's solution. Instead, you want a quick, direct route. Further, if your audience is a conservative client, judge, or colleague, you do not want a risky route that breaks new ground. Rather, you want a familiar, traditional route. The point is that you have to put all of the pieces together to decide what kind of a road map you want to prepare in any given matter.

EXAMPLE

Here is a simple example that illustrates the where, what, why, who, when, and how template in the context of an actual road map from which we will draw some comparisons to legal writing.

Suppose that you have an out-of-town visitor. The visitor would like to see a movie. The local movie theater is two miles from your home. You write down for the visitor the following directions:

> ➤ From my house, go north three blocks to the highway.
> ➤ Go east on the highway and get off at the Main Street exit.
> ➤ At the end of the exit, go straight on the frontage road.
> ➤ In about half a block, turn into the movie theater parking lot.

These directions may well get your visitor to the movie theater. But ask yourself the where, what, why, who, when, and how questions. You might discover that the directions are wrong, or that they could be improved.

The visitor wants to go to see a movie. *What* movie? Any particular movie, or just whatever happens to be playing? This makes a difference. If the visitor wants to see the latest *Star Wars* adventure, and that movie is not at the local theater, you have just given your visitor a useless set of directions. Worse, not only are the directions useless, but the visitor will be affirmatively angry to arrive at the destination to discover that the movie is not playing there. You must know with some precision what the goal is before you give directions.

Why does the visitor want to see a movie, and why do you want to select the local theater as the destination? Does the visitor simply want to find a way to pass the time on a lazy afternoon? Does the visitor hope to learn something? Do you want to show off the mall where the theater is located? The answers make a difference because, again, maybe you just directed the visitor to the wrong place. Maybe the visitor who wants to learn something would rather go to the theater at the local science museum and wander through the exhibits after watching a movie there. Maybe the biggest mall in America is ten miles away and is even more spectacular than the local mall.

Who is the visitor? Has she visited before? Has she been to the local movie theater before? Will she know what direction is north? Will she know what the "highway" is? Even assuming that the local movie theater is exactly the correct place to send the visitor, will she be lost as a result of your directions?

Turning to the *when* question, you may wonder about timing. If the movie the visitor wants to see is indeed playing at the local mall, the movie starts in ten minutes, and the visitor needs to be back at your house in no later than two and one-half hours, then sending the visitor to the movie theater two miles away is a good choice. The destination is a correct one because the visitor is in a hurry.

But suppose the visitor simply wants to find a way to spend a lazy afternoon. The visitor does not care what time the movie starts: She is indifferent as among the 1:00, 3:00, and 5:00 shows. She would be happy to see some local landmarks before the movie. Then what is the point of sending your visitor by the fastest possible route to the nearest mall?

Finally, asking the *how* question demonstrates that the four-point set of directions leaves out information that a clear set of directions should contain. To begin, there is no title. If the visitor puts the directions in a pocket where there are other notes of directions to other places, she will not immediately know which writing tells her how to get to the movies.

The first instruction is ambiguous. It tells the visitor to go "north" three blocks to the "highway." Is north to the right or to the left out of your driveway? Is the "highway" State Highway 56, or County Highway 20, both of which pass through your neighborhood approximately three blocks from your house? A much clearer first direction would be, "When you leave my house, turn right up my street (Washington St.), and go three blocks to the State Highway 56 entrance ramp."

moral - be specific

The second instruction is also potentially ambiguous. It tells the visitor to go "east" on the highway to the Main Street exit. Presumably that means a right turn onto the highway, because the visitor has previously been traveling north. But why not make that explicit? And will the Main Street exit be so labeled, or will the exit sign say "Highway 7," because that is another designation for "Main Street"? A much clearer instruction would be, "Turn right just after you pass the ABC gas station, and follow the sign for East Highway 56. Go 1.2 miles on Highway 56, stay in the right lane, and go up the exit ramp for Main Street (= Highway 7)."

You can improve even the third instruction. The visitor may not know what you mean by the "frontage road." Spell this out: "At the end of the exit ramp, do not turn on Main Street. Instead, go straight ahead through the Main Street traffic light. You will be on the frontage road that parallels Highway 56."

Finally, you can improve the fourth instruction. The movie theater is in the local mall. The mall has a name, "Main Street Mall," and a large sign at its entrance. Give the visitor those landmarks by saying, "Go half a block to the large Main Street Mall sign, turn right into the Mall parking lot, and look for the movie theater straight ahead across the parking lot."

Certain general principles can be distilled from the above example:

➢ Use titles so your reader can tell the destination at the outset.

➢ Do not assume prior knowledge; spell out the terms you are using.

> ➤ Refer to landmarks as a guide to progress.

> ➤ Be precise.

> ➤ Make sure the directions are in proper sequence.

COMPARISON TO LEGAL WRITING

Suppose now an assignment to prepare a "legal road map" in the case of *Bears v. Gold.* The following are the basic facts (adapted from the well-known children's story)[4]:

A twelve year-old girl named Sarah Gold became lost in the woods. She eventually stumbled upon a house as night was falling. She went up to the front door and knocked. When nobody answered, she opened the door, which was unlocked, and went inside after brushing her feet off on the mat on the front porch.

To the right of the entrance hall was the dining room. On the table were three bowls of vegetarian chili. "Wow," said Sarah, "food!" She sat down at the table and began to eat. "That hurt," exclaimed Sarah, as she sampled the first bowl. "Too hot!" Sarah pulled over the second bowl. "Yuck," she said, "too cold." So Sarah turned to the third bowl. "Just right," she said. She gobbled it down, because she was ravenously hungry.

Once she had eaten supper, she realized she was frightfully tired. So she lay down on the sofa in the living room and fell fast asleep.

In the morning, she awoke with the sunrise. She did the dishes and left, after leaving a note that said, "Thanks for

---

[4] One of the authors has previously used a version of the Bears problem at a Minnesota State Bar Association CLE workshop for appellate lawyers.

the food and the good night sleep. I would have paid you, but I am lost and have no money with me. Sarah Gold."

Sarah eventually found her way home. A month later, however, a process server confronted her with a summons and complaint. Robert, Barbara, and Bert Bear are suing Sarah for trespass.

Ignore for the moment whether your road map will ultimately take the form of an office memorandum, a client letter, or a brief for a court. We will describe those specific templates in later chapters. Focus instead on the simple road map basics. Assume for the moment that you are the lawyer for Sarah and that you are going to argue that Sarah's actions are justified by an "emergency" defense. Further assume that you have conducted research and interviewed Sarah. Here is your roadmap:

Roadmap	Explanation
Robert Bear, Barbara Bear, and Bert Bear **v.** **Sarah Gold**	Case caption (which in a formal legal document would include the names of the parties, the court, the case number, and the title of the document).
Defense theory for Sarah: Emergency	Title of the road map.
Goal: Dismissal of the Complaint; threshold motion to dismiss for failure of the Complaint to state a viable legal claim based on the facts pleaded.	Identification of the destination: the overall *where* and *what* questions and answers.
Basic equation for why dismissal is proper: Need to encourage assistance to travelers in emergencies; need to encourage assistance to children in emergencies; only nominal "damage" to Bear family in this case; on balance, society's interest in protecting Sarah outweighs interest in	Identification of the *why* question and answer.

protecting Bears under the circumstances.	
<u>Audience</u>: The client for now; ultimately, the court.	Identification of the _who_ question and answer.
<u>Timing</u>: File the motion as soon as possible to prevent client from incurring unnecessary legal fees in broader defense of case.	Identification of the _when_ question and answer.
<u>Basis for the motion in detail</u>:	
➤ Issue: Whether Sarah can be liable for trespass onto the Bears' property when she entered it in an emergency.	Identification of the _how_ question and answer.
➤ Conclusion: No, emergency is a complete defense.	
➤ Legal rule: The Moot State Supreme Court has decided six cases involving an emergency defense to a trespass claim. In three cases involving children in trouble, the court upheld the defense and found no liability on the part of the child-trespasser. (In one of those three cases, an eleven-year-old child entered a person's home in a forest to obtain shelter in an electric storm.) In two cases involving adults who were not genuinely in trouble, the court rejected the defense and found liability. In one case involving a child who pretended there was an emergency to gain access to the property for the purpose of playing a prank, the court rejected the defense and found liability.	Within the _how_ question, road map the _who, what, where, when, why,_ and _how_ sub-questions that tell the story AND identify the legal rule that will apply.
➤ Factual story: Sarah is twelve years old and still a child. At the time of the "trespass," she was lost in the woods. Night was falling. Dangerous animals, including wolves, prowl the forest at dusk, looking for prey. She entered the Bear family's house across a front porch mat that said, "welcome." The door was unlocked. She knocked first, but entered upon	

hearing rustling noises in the bushes behind her. She played no pranks on the Bear family. ➤ Application of the law to the facts: The present case is like the three previous cases in which the court found no liability. It is particularly like the electric storm shelter case. ➤ Requested solution: Dismiss the Bears' Complaint.	

CONCLUSION

The kind of road mapping provided in this exercise is very helpful in working through a difficult legal question. We encourage you to think about this approach each time you are parsing through a problem that needs a solution.

CHAPTER 2

The Role of Facts
In Resolving Legal Problems

> **Just the facts, ma'am, just the facts.**
>
> Jack Webb as Sgt. Joe Friday, *Dragnet*
> (NBC 1952-1959, 1967-1970) (TV series).

There was a popular television show in the 1950s and late 1960s known as *Dragnet*. It was a police detective drama, starring Jack Webb. In virtually every episode, or at least the ones we can remember, Webb would knock on the door of a potential witness, typically a woman, who would answer the knock and ask something like, "What would you like to know, officer?" Webb would reply laconically, "Just the facts, ma'am, just the facts."

The writers for the show had the right idea. What matters in police investigations are the facts. Similarly, facts matter first and foremost in legal analysis and writing.

Facts are the driving force behind legal problems. If you do not understand the relevant factual story with which you are dealing, then you do not really understand what legal principles might, will, or should apply to the problem you are addressing. The common law develops through a series of individual court decisions, each one of which addresses a single problem for a single set of parties. It is only by looking at the material fact patterns across the decided cases that a lawyer figures out how a court might, will, or should view the problem in the client's present case. Similarly, statutory law develops through a series of legislative enactments, each one of which addresses a category of fact problem confronting multiple persons (civil rights issues, employment difficulties, environmental concerns, etc.). It is only by looking at the facts behind the legislative problem that a lawyer figures out how a court might, will, or should apply the statute to the client's present case.

Curiously, this can be an easy concept to forget. It is easy to become embroiled in learning "the law" (read: rules), without considering that legal principles serve to solve problems, and problems arise because of facts. From a practicing lawyer's standpoint, "the law" is not an abstract set of rules. Lawyers do not simply look up a legal rule in a book, provide the court, client, or adversary with the rule, and then expect to get paid large sums of money. If that was all there is to the practice of law, then courts, clients, and adversaries would just look up the rules themselves. No, there is much more. The rest of this chapter focuses on the identification of the facts that give rise to legal problems.

STORY IDENTIFICATION

At the outset, remember that a lawyer is not analyzing or writing fiction. She does not get to make up the facts.[1] She gets to discover them.

---

[1] There is a quasi exception to this statement: A client may come to a lawyer to seek assistance in connection with events that are still unfolding. For example, the client may be negotiating a transaction that has not concluded. Or the client may be jockeying for position in a potential dispute that has not yet fully matured. In these kinds of settings, the lawyer is not creating fiction, but the lawyer is helping to create the real facts of the story as events move forward. Most first-year law students will be working on problems where the material facts already exist, and the students are to identify and analyze them. But rejoice if you get the chance to work on a scenario in real-time, where you get to help create the story pro-actively as it unfolds.

That is a digging process. The lawyer reads. The lawyer talks to people. The lawyer searches for data. The lawyer does what a good investigative reporter does: She looks for "who, what, where, when, why, and how."

And do not assume that all of the facts will be readily available or come tumbling out of sources such as the lawyer's client. Sources do not always recognize the materiality of specific facts. Sometimes, even when the source does recognize the materiality, the source does not want to volunteer the facts because the source perceives they are unfavorable. It is the lawyer's job to investigate, and to investigate hard.

Let's break out the factual analysis in the *Bears v. Gold* case to illustrate the process. Recall the basic picture from Chapter 1:

> A twelve-year-old girl named Sarah Gold became lost in the woods. She eventually stumbled upon a house as night was falling. She went up to the front door and knocked. When nobody answered, she opened the door, which was unlocked, and went inside after brushing her feet off on the mat on the front porch.

> To the right of the entrance hall was the dining room. On the table were three bowls of vegetarian chili. "Wow," said Sarah, "food!" She sat down at the table and began to eat. "That hurt," exclaimed Sarah, as she sampled the first bowl. "Too hot!" Sarah pulled over the second bowl. "Yuck," she said, "too cold." So Sarah turned to the third bowl. "Just right," she said. She gobbled it down, because she was ravenously hungry.

> Once she had eaten supper, she realized she was frightfully tired. So she lay down on the sofa in the living room and fell fast asleep.

> In the morning, she awoke with the sunrise. She did the dishes and left, after leaving a note that said, "Thanks for the food and the good night sleep. I would have paid you, but I am lost and have no money with me. Sarah Gold."

Sarah eventually found her way home. A month later, however, a process server confronted her with a summons and complaint. Robert, Barbara, and Bert Bear are suing Sarah for trespass.

Sarah and her parents have now hired you to represent them in the lawsuit.[2] They want to know if this is a frivolous case. Before you answer, what would you need to know?

Your first instinct might be to look up the current rules of the law of trespass in your jurisdiction. Undoubtedly, you will want to research those rules, and undoubtedly once you research those rules you will want to re-look at the facts, and then probably re-look at the rules. (Remember: there are lots of starts and stops, detours, and back-and-forth efforts. The process is messy.) But before you begin looking up "the law," think about the material facts you know and the ones you do not know.

First, what do you know and what do you not know so far about the *who* in the story? You know that your client is twelve years old. Trespass is an intentional tort. Can a twelve-year-old form the requisite intent? How precocious is Sarah? Did *this* twelve-year-old form the requisite intent?

By the same token, *who* is the Bear family? Do the Bears run a bed and breakfast place? Does the mat on the front porch read, "Bear B & B; Welcome all visitors"? Or did Sarah wander into the Bears' private home? Does the mat on the front porch read, "Beware of Bears"?

Do the Bear family and Sarah know each other? Is there any prior history of animosity? Alternatively, is there any prior history of accommodation?

Second, what do you know and what do you not know about the *when* in the story? You know that night was falling at the time of the house entry. Were the woods getting dark? Were the house lights on? What kinds of

---

[2] Because Sarah is a minor, her parents would assume defense of the case, in the real world. The case caption might read, "Robert Bear, Barbara Bear, and Bert Bear v. Sarah Gold, a minor, by her parents, John Gold and Susan Gold."

animals roam this forest at night? Did Sarah become afraid for her safety? Did nightfall create an emergency in her mind? Was she under duress?

Third, what do you know and what do you not know about the *where* in the story? You know that Sarah came upon the door in the middle of the forest and that it was unlocked. Did Sarah take the unlocked door as an indicator of consent to enter? Did Sarah have to climb over a locked fence gate to get to the porch in the first place? Is there a common understanding in the forest relating to the freedom of visitors to enter buildings to rest?

Fourth, what do you know and what do you not know about the *what* in the story? You know that Sarah knocked on the front door, entered the building, ate some vegetarian chili, slept on the sofa, did the dishes, and departed without leaving cash. Was the knock a sign of respect, a polite act, or a sign that Sarah knew she needed permission to enter the building? And what about the dishes? Did Sarah intend to offer doing the dishes as a form of payment for the chili and the night's sleep, in lieu of cash? Does the note she left help in that regard or does it hurt? What else did she do? For example, did she drop the hot bowl on the floor when she picked it up from the table? Did the bowl break? Did she leave a mess on the floor for the Bears to clean?

Fifth, what do you know and what do you not know about the *why* in the story? What motivated Sarah? Fear? Exhaustion? Hunger? For that matter, what is motivating the Bears? Saving face among the other bears? Greed? Frustration?

Finally, what do you know and what do you not know about the *how* in the story? How did Sarah act? She seems to have been respectful. Was she really?[3]

Without knowing the answers to the above fact questions, you do not know what legal principles might be relevant to solving the clients' problem, namely ending the lawsuit favorably. You do not know how to compare your case to others that have involved trespass. You might conceivably be interested in a number of different potential legal defenses, including lack of

---

[3] Notice, by the way, after becoming a law student, how you may never look at life the same way again. We suspect that many of you have not previously thought of children's stories as involving potential lawsuits.

relevant intent, existence of an emergency, duress, consent, and payment. The facts come first, then the law.

ADDITIONAL STORY IDENTIFICATION PRINCIPLES

As you formulate an understanding of the who, what, where, when, why, and how facts of a story, you should also have in mind the following related principles.

1. While gathering the facts, make sure to assemble the beginning, the middle, and the end to the story. Think about the relationships among the *who, what, where, when, why,* and *how* pieces. Do they fit together? Do they make sense as a whole? Are they clear? Can a person begin in place x, travel through place y, and wind up in place z when you put all of the pieces side-by-side? At the end of the day, can you put together a coherent solution to the problem presented by the story?

2. Recognize and account for all the material facts in the story. It is hard to assemble a good story with incomplete facts. It is especially hard to solve a legal problem when operating with incomplete facts. Test and re-test your understanding to make sure you are finding and accounting for all material information. And if you have to offer a tentative solution to a legal problem before you believe you have all the material facts, consider how you will tell your audience what is missing that might affect your solution.

3. Think about what in the story makes it interesting. Good stories are not dull. Admittedly, when an author is not writing fiction, the author cannot invent untrue facts just for the sake of creating a good story. Lawyers live with the facts they have. But no legal problem is dull. Legal stories are inherently interesting because by definition they involve some kind of clash among people and ideas. So focus on the facts that produced the clash. Ask yourself: As I assemble the *who, what, where, when, why,* and *how* pieces of the story I am analyzing, what about each piece makes it intriguing?

4. Think about the context for the story. Legal problems do not exist in a vacuum. They arise in the context of a society that has a history, customs, values, attitudes, and policies. Legal stories are inextricably intertwined with all of those. Do not forget to think about the *who, what,* *where, when, why*, and *how* of your specific story within the broader context in which that story takes place.

CONCLUSION

In Chapters 11 and 12, you will see some examples of fact statements for different audiences. For now, we want you simply to understand how important it is for you to dig for and analyze the facts giving rise to legal problems. Those facts drive everything else.

CHAPTER 3

The Role of Rules
in Resolving Legal Problems

To resolve legal problems, lawyers must be able to identify the appropriate rules that will be applied to the facts—or the story. To identify the appropriate rules requires an understanding of the sources of rules—or authority—and the hierarchy of authority. Discussions of authority necessarily involve jurisdictional issues, which can be a very complex area of the law. An in-depth discussion of jurisdiction is more properly taken up in such courses as conflicts of laws and federal jurisdiction. Our purpose in this chapter is two-fold. First, we want to acquaint you with the basics regarding sources of rules and hierarchy of authority, which you will need in order to work through your legal writing problems. Second, we want to provide you with enough detail to convey the potential complexity of jurisdictional issues.

THE SOURCES OF RULES:
ENACTED LAW AND CASES

Broadly speaking, the rules that lawyers identify and apply to resolve a legal problem come from primary authority. Primary authority consists of enacted laws and cases. ***Enacted law*** is defined here to include constitutions (which are more typically adopted by representative bodies), statutes (which are enacted by legislative bodies), and administrative rules and regulations (which are promulgated by administrative agencies). ***Cases*** are the written reports of decisions by judicial bodies—or courts. Case law is further divided into cases that interpret enacted law and common law cases. These sources of law exist at the federal and state level.

Sources of Primary Authority	
Federal	**State**
Constitution	Constitution
Statutes	Statutes
Administrative Rules and Regulations	Administrative Rules and Regulations Local: Municipal Charters and Ordinances

Cases:
    Interpretive (of enacted law)
    Common Law
	Cases:
	    Interpretive (of enacted law)
	    Common Law

1. Enacted Law

The United States Constitution is the source of our federal system of government. The Constitution is the highest law in the United States. In other words, legislative bodies—federal and state—may not enact rules that are inconsistent with the federal constitution. Courts determine whether a statute or regulation is unconstitutional.[1] The United States Supreme Court is the highest and final authority on federal constitutional issues. The individual states also have constitutions, and the state's court of last resort is the highest authority with

---

[1] The doctrine of judicial review was first announced by the United States Supreme Court in *Marbury v. Madison*, 5 U.S. 137 (1803).

respect to interpreting the state's constitution. If, however, there is a federal constitutional challenge to a provision in a state constitution, the United States Supreme Court would have final authority with respect to whether that provision violated the federal constitution.

Statutes are typically more specific than constitutions, although some constitutional provisions can be quite specific. Statutes are general statements of the law and usually prescribe or proscribe specific conduct in a particular area across a class of persons. There are several reasons why a legislative body may decide to enact statutes. For example, there may be a generic problem that the legislature wants to address, such as environmental protection, or a specific problem, such as permitting electronic signatures. Additionally, the legislature may want to provide a framework of rules for the conduct of certain activity, such as the sale of goods, which is governed in 49 states by their enactment of Article 2 of the *Uniform Commercial Code*. Further, the legislature may want to clarify an ambiguity created by case law or enact legislation to change—or abrogate— the common law.

Statutes often need to be interpreted by courts. For example, sometimes the court must determine the meaning of a particular provision. At other times, the court must determine if the statute is constitutional—either under the federal or a state constitution. There is a wealth of material available to the lawyer when advocating a particular meaning or construction of a federal statute because of the vast number of documents created in passing the legislation. There are fewer documents at the state level when interpreting state statutes, but some do exist. (Learning how to find these documents and the relative value of each of them in relation to each other will likely be taken up in the research component of your research and writing course. Learning how to use these documents as a problem solver is the subject of Chapter 7.)

For our purposes, it is important to note that courts routinely interpret statutes. As discussed above, the United States Supreme Court is the final authority on the federal constitutionality of any federal or state statute. The state court of last resort is the highest authority with respect to interpreting a state statute in accordance with state law.[2] In fact, if a federal court is interpreting a

---

[2] State courts do address the federal constitutionality of state statutes, but they are not the final authority. The U.S. Supreme Court is.

substantive state law in a diversity action, the federal court must look to how that state's highest court has interpreted—or would interpret—the provision.[3] If the state's highest court has not spoken on the issue, then the federal court must try to discern how the state court would decide.[4] And if the state court subsequently addresses the same issue, it is not bound by the federal court opinion, although the federal opinion would typically be persuasive.

At this point, it is important to understand that the lawyer as problem solver must master two systems of government—federal and state. Further, at the federal level, each of the circuits functions as a distinct jurisdiction; and at the state level, each state is a separate jurisdiction. The federal and state governmental systems are at times parallel; at other times they overlap and the lawyer must determine which jurisdiction's rule applies. (This can also be said of determining which state's rule applies in some situations.) As a general principle, if there is a conflict between a federal statute and a state statute, the federal statute trumps the state statute, assuming Congress intended to preempt that area of law and that Congress has the constitutional authority to govern that subject. (This is an overly simplified discussion of this topic. We assume it will be explained in greater detail in the research component of your research and writing course, or in your civil procedure and constitutional law courses.)

Administrative rules and regulations are generally promulgated by federal and state administrative agencies. They are typically even more specific than statutes. Administrative law—at the federal and state level—is highly complex. The weight given to a rule, as well as to the interpretation of the rule by the agency or a court, can vary. Consequently, when confronted with an administrative law problem, it is essential to read the statute that created the specific agency.

---

[3] *Erie R.R. Co. v. Tompkins*, 304 U.S. 64, 58 S. Ct. 817 (1938). More specifically, a federal court sitting in diversity must apply state substantive law—either statutory or common law. (Note that most uniform systems of citation do not require a parallel citation to *United States Reports*. West publications include a citation to *Supreme Court Reporter* for U.S. Supreme Court cases.)

[4] State courts ascertaining federal law in the absence of a United States Supreme Court decision have not been uniform in their approaches. Donald H. Zeigler, *Gazing into the Crystal Ball: Reflections on the Standards State Judges Should Use to Ascertain Federal Law*, 40 Wm. & Mary L. Rev. 1143, 1143 (1999).

2. *Cases*

> There are two categories of cases:
> interpretive and common law.

Cases, like enacted laws, are primary authority. There are two categories of cases: interpretive and common law. The definition of interpretive cases should by now be obvious to you: cases in which courts *interpret* enacted law. The definition also encompasses those cases in which courts *apply* enacted law. In other words, it may not be necessary for the court to interpret a particular provision; instead, the court is ruling on how the law should—or should not—be applied to a particular set of facts. For example, where a term is ambiguous, the court will need to interpret that term, relying on canons of statutory construction or the legislative history, or both. Some terms are not ambiguous in themselves, such as the term "reasonable." But determining what is reasonable in a specific situation requires a fact-specific analysis, comparing and contrasting the instant facts with the facts of similar cases. Other statutory provisions or terms may only need to be applied. If the statute states, "Where a tender has been accepted . . . the buyer must within a reasonable time after he discovers or should have discovered any breach notify the seller of the breach or be barred from any remedy . . . ,"[5] and the buyer did not notify the seller, then the court would apply the rule. The buyer would be precluded from pursuing a remedy for a breach by the seller. If the buyer sent notice, then there may be an issue as to whether the notice was sent in a reasonable time, which would require comparing and contrasting cases in which notice was sent.

Another form of case law is the common law. It is based on the concept of precedent. Precedent can be described as coming from custom or habit.[6] Some would say that the common law, or the precedent, is discovered—not created.[7] The United States is considered a common law country, having a

---

[5] U.C.C. § 2-607(3)(a) (1994).

[6] Karl N. Llewellyn, *The Bramble Bush* 70 (Oceana 1960).

[7] In fact, judges do create law while applying precedent to resolve a particular legal problem. J. Myron Jacobstein et al., *Fundamentals of Legal Research* 4-5 (7th ed., Found. Press 1998).

system of law brought by the first settlers from England. English common law was, and continues to be, albeit much less so, precedent for the courts in this country.[8]

> Like cases should be treated
> alike.

The doctrine of precedent has a strong ethical component that dates back to Aristotle: Like cases should be treated alike.[9] Many of the cases you will read during your first-year courses will be common law cases.

Under the common law, the rules—or precedent—evolve from the cases themselves. In other words, there is no statute. And, unlike statutes, common law cases are resolutions to specific problems between specific parties. These cases tend to be fact specific. In time, however, when later courts apply a case as precedent to subsequent cases with similar—or seemingly similar—facts, general common law rules evolve. The common law rule that the acceptance must be the mirror image of the offer in contract law is but one example.

Sometimes common law rules become codified. For example, the contract damages rules announced in *Hadley v. Baxendale*, 156 Eng. Rep. 145 (Ex. 1854), were codified when legislatures enacted Sections 2-714 and 2-715 of the *Uniform Commercial Code*. Or legislatures may enact laws that abrogate—or displace—the common law. The common law mirror-image rule mentioned above was abrogated by Section 2-207 of the *Uniform Commercial Code*. And here is an important point to remember when working with authority: statutes trump the common law within a specific jurisdiction. Even though courts are the mechanism for interpreting and applying enacted law, legislatures have the power to enact laws that abrogate the common law.

---

[8] You will read a very famous English case, *Hadley v. Baxendale*, 156 Eng. Rep. 145 (Ex. 1854), in your contracts course that established the rules for contract damages.

[9] *See* Aristotle, *Nicomachean Ethics* b. 5, ch. 4.

> Predictability is critical for the
> problem solver.

Just as facts are the driving force in identifying legal problems, primary authority is the driving force in resolving legal problems. The complex system of enacted law and case law both promotes predictability and provides for needed change. Predictability is critical for the problem solver. Without some degree of stability, we would be unable to conduct our lives and business affairs in an orderly, rational fashion. Without some degree of stability, lawyers would not be able to advise clients. Predictability in the law, however, is not the same as a guaranty. Sometimes the law is so clear on its face that you can predict with a high degree of certainty, but often it is not.[10]

At the same time, the system allows for needed change. Legislatures repeal unnecessary legislation and enact necessary legislation. Courts narrow— even overrule—precedent as conditions change that once made that particular precedent useful or desirable. And within this system, the lawyer often has room to maneuver. Much of your first year in law school will be devoted to learning how to parse a case broadly and narrowly.

BASIC PRINCIPLES FOR UNDERSTANDING PRIMARY AUTHORITY

Primary authority is classified as mandatory, persuasive, or not applicable even though on point. Not knowing when the authority is mandatory or persuasive or not applicable could lead to disastrous results. You may give your client the wrong advice, or you may argue rules or cases that have no applicability to your problem even though they are on point. Here are some basic principles for understanding how to classify the authority. The key to understanding the differences is in understanding the role jurisdiction plays. But first, some definitions. *Mandatory* means the courts within that jurisdiction are bound by the enacted rule or precedent. *Persuasive* means the courts may look to the source in helping them to decide a particular issue. *Not applicable*, even

---

[10] A caveat: a client should always be advised in terms of predictabilities; do not guarantee an outcome. Juries and judges occasionally misapply the law—that is, they act irrationally or inconsistently with the stated rule or precedent.

though on point, means just that. The source may be the perfect statute, or a great case applying that statute, but the source cannot be applied in your jurisdiction because your jurisdiction has not enacted that statute.

1. State constitutions and statutes are either mandatory or not applicable. The constitution and statutes from one state are mandatory—or binding—on the state law problems and claims arising in that state. They have no persuasive value on other states. In other words, it would be impermissible to argue in a case involving Michigan law that the Michigan Supreme Court should apply a statute from Wyoming.

However, and this is a big however, if one jurisdiction has the same or a very similar statute as another jurisdiction, the *cases* interpreting those provisions are persuasive to other courts. (The same would be true of constitutional provisions.) To illustrate, assume State A and State B have both enacted Article 2 of the *Uniform Commercial Code*. Further assume that the courts of State A have not interpreted a particular provision that is at issue in a case before the court. The judicial opinions of State B (and any other state that has interpreted the same enacted provision) are persuasive authority.[11]   The same is true between federal and state legislation, i.e., state constitutions and statutes do not resolve federal legal questions, and vice versa. But assume that State A has enacted rules of evidence that closely mirror the federal rules of evidence. If the courts of State A must interpret a particular rule, the opinions of the federal courts interpreting the same rule in the federal system will be highly persuasive.

2. Enacted law trumps the common law within a specific jurisdiction. As mentioned above, the legislature of a specific jurisdiction can modify or abrogate a common law rule. This is because legislation is an expression of the will of the people in that state. Consequently, if you are resolving a problem within a specific jurisdiction, which in practice you would be, you must first determine if there is enacted law that governs the problem. If the legislature has not spoken, then you would determine if the highest court of that state has addressed the issue. If the highest court and the inferior appellate courts have not

---

[11] There are, of course, some nuances to this basic principle. For example, greater weight is usually given to states whose courts routinely address this type of issue. Moreover, individual states may have rules or practices to determine which jurisdictions' judicial opinions the court will consider.

addressed the issue, then you would search the common law of other states. But you would not search the statutes of other states (except in the circumstances stated in 1). This is because the common law is said to belong to everyone. Thus, a state court is free to look to the common law of other states, but it is not free to adopt legislation that other jurisdictions have enacted. Courts do not enact legislation.

3. Cases can be mandatory, persuasive, or not applicable. The only part of a mandatory case that is mandatory—or binding—is where the court is announcing the rule of law with respect to the dispute before it—the holding—and even then it is only binding on the inferior courts within that jurisdiction.[12] All other parts of the opinion are considered persuasive, even within a mandatory case as defined above. This includes dicta (general statements by the court not necessary to the holding but which may be highly persuasive), concurring opinions, and dissenting opinions. All of these parts of the case may be cited as authority, but they must be properly attributed and treated as only persuasive.

To determine if the rule of the case is mandatory requires knowing whether the case was decided by a court within the specific jurisdiction that governs your problem and whether the case addresses the same issue. The first question is whether the case is binding in your jurisdiction with respect to the kind of legal problem at issue. The second question is, within a binding case, what part of the discussion is mandatory. In other words, does the doctrine of stare decisis apply? Stare decisis means that the precedent is mandatory—or binding—in that jurisdiction. For example, under the federal system involving a federal issue, the Federal District Court for the Eastern District of Michigan is bound by all the decisions of the Court of Appeals for the Sixth Circuit and the decisions of the United States Supreme Court. Decisions from other federal courts of appeal are persuasive, but not mandatory. Similarly, the Sixth Circuit Court of Appeals is bound by the decisions of the United States Supreme Court on federal issues. But the opinions of its sister courts of appeal are not mandatory, only persuasive.

At the state level, the inferior courts are bound by all the decisions of the

---

[12] Some state appellate courts are bound by the decisions of other appellate panels within that state. Therefore, it is always important to check that state's court rules.

highest state court on matters of state law. However, on matters of federal law, the state courts are bound by the decisions of the United States Supreme Court.[13] And the federal courts are bound by the decisions of the highest state courts on purely state issues.

> Secondary authority is never binding.

4. If the authority is not primary, then it is secondary, which may be persuasive but is never binding. Secondary authority includes all other expressions of the law, such as Restatements, treatises, law review articles, and monographs. These are all sources to use in resolving the problem and communicating the analysis. Other sources such as legal dictionaries, legal encyclopedias, *American Law Reports*, and various case-finding tools, such as digests, are often useful in helping to locate or identify the potentially appropriate rules. All secondary authority is not equal in that greater weight is given to some secondary sources than others. Moreover, a court is always free to ignore secondary authority.

CONSIDERATIONS WHEN WORKING WITH STATUTES AND CASES

Being able to resolve a legal problem requires understanding not just the sources of rules, but how to work with them. Below we provide general considerations in working with statutes and cases, followed by a basic template for organizing your approach to identifying the correct sources to resolve a legal problem.

---

[13] There is a split of authority among the state courts as to whether they are bound by lower federal court decisions on issues of federal law. Zeigler, *supra* n. 4, at 1151.

Working with Statutes

First, statutes regulate human conduct. Identify when the conduct is always regulated and when it is regulated only at specified times.

Second, statutes are best understood as imperative statements that command, prohibit, or permit specific conduct.

Third, courts presume when interpreting statutes that the drafters intended to create a consistent and coherent body of law. Therefore, courts will resist any interpretation of one portion of a statute that negates or contradicts another section of the statute.

Fourth, statutes have a discernable structure. Pay close attention to the definitions, the language used, the punctuation, and how the parts of the statute relate to one another.

Working with Cases

First, understand that there are two ways to read a case as a lawyer. One is as a historical event where the court resolved a specific dispute between specific parties involving specific facts. The second is to determine its viability as precedent for predicting how a court would decide a case involving the same issue on similar facts. It is the latter with which you will be most concerned as a problem solver. Whenever possible, read the cases in relation to the problem you are trying to resolve.

Second, appreciate that cases tell a story. Determine which facts of the story each court relied on in arriving at its conclusion. Look carefully at the court's reasoning. Determine the factual similarities and dissimilarities in subsequent decisions and their importance to the outcome.[14]

Third, formulate the rule from the case or cases broadly and narrowly. Ask how much the case or cases can be made to stand for and how little.[15] (Much more will be said about how to formulate rules from cases in Chapters 4 through 6.)

---

[14] Llewellyn, *supra* n. 7, at 49.

[15] *Id.* at 73-74; Soia Mentschikoff & Irwin P. Stotzky, *The Theory and Craft of American Law* xxxi-xxxii (Matthew Bender 1992).

Basic Template for Identifying Sources to Resolve Legal Problems

Organize your approach to a legal problem by reference to the source(s) of law that will govern the result:

First, ask: Is the problem one of federal law or state law (or both)?

Second, ask: Within the category of federal or state law, is the problem governed by enacted law or common law?

Third, ask: If enacted law governs, then within the category of federal enacted law or state enacted law, what kind of enacted law applies—a constitution? A statute? An administrative regulation?

Fourth, ask: If enacted law governs, and court decisions interpret the enacted law, which cases are binding in your jurisdiction on the legal issues you face? (Cases that are not binding in your jurisdiction can never be more than merely persuasive or simply not applicable.)

Fifth, ask: Within the binding cases interpreting the enacted law, what parts of the opinion are mandatory and what parts are merely persuasive?

Sixth, ask: If common law rather than enacted law governs, then which common law cases are binding in your jurisdiction on the legal issues you face? (Cases that are not binding in your jurisdiction can never be more than persuasive.)

Seventh, ask: Within the binding common law cases, what parts of the opinions are mandatory and what parts are merely persuasive?

Eighth, ask: If there is no binding authority, which jurisdictions' treatment of the problem will you select as most persuasive?

CHAPTER 4

Determining the Rule
in Typical, Simple Scenarios

Lawyers spend their entire careers working with rules. In Chapter 3, we discussed the role of rules in resolving legal problems. In this chapter, we discuss how to disassemble and assemble rules.

PULLING APART A RULE

We begin by breaking apart one of the Minnesota Rules of Professional Conduct (2002).[1] It might seem strange to begin by disassembling a rule instead of assembling one. But disassembly of a rule to see how its elements might apply to resolve a legal problem is part of your ultimate endgame; so we want you to see the disassembly process as a predicate for your work with rules generally. While we focus here on a

---

[1] The Minnesota Rules of Professional Conduct are similar if not identical to the American Bar Association Model Rules. Accordingly, readers in other jurisdictions can likely find the same basic rule in their own state. Careful readers will notice that this book cites to a number of Minnesota and Michigan authorities as examples. The authors are familiar with the illustrative value of those authorities after many years of practice and teaching. You can find similar authorities in other jurisdictions.

statutory rule, the same process of parsing applies equally to those common rules that are composed of elements.

Minnesota Rule 3.7(a):

    (a) A lawyer shall not act as advocate at a trial in which the lawyer is likely to be a necessary witness unless:

    1. the testimony relates to an uncontested issue;
    2. the testimony relates to the nature and value of legal services rendered in the case; or
    3. disqualification of the lawyer would work substantial hardship on the client.

How many elements does this rule contain? One potential answer would be three, but that is a gross understatement. There are at least twenty-five elements.

Outline of the Elements of Minnesota Rule 3.7 (a):	Commentary on the Outline of the Elements of Rule 3.7 (a):
➢ A lawyer ➢ shall not act ➢ as advocate ➢ at a trial ➢ in which ➢ the lawyer ➢ is likely to be ➢ a necessary ➢ witness	The introductory language to Rule 3.7(a) contains nine discrete elements. You need all nine of those elements present *or you never get to* "unless (1)," "unless (2)," or "unless (3)":
	The rule only applies to lawyers. It involves a prohibition. The lawyer cannot act as an advocate. When? At trial. What kind of a trial? One in which the lawyer will be a witness. What kind of a witness? A likely one. Is that all? A likely, necessary witness.
➢ unless: ➢ the testimony ➢ relates to	So you are into *who, what, where, when, why,* and *how* questions again. If your problem does not involve a lawyer, Rule 3.7(a) is not applicable. If your problem does not involve a trial, the rule is not applicable. If the lawyer is not going to be a witness

➢ an uncontested
➢ issue;
      OR
➢ the testimony
➢ relates to
➢ the nature and
➢ the value of
➢ legal services
➢ rendered in the case;
      OR
➢ disqualification
➢ of the lawyer
➢ would work substantial
➢ hardship
➢ on the client.
	in the trial, the rule is not applicable. If the lawyer is not likely to be a witness in the trial, the rule is not applicable. If the lawyer is likely to be a witness, but not a necessary witness, the rule is not applicable.
	
	Assume that all nine of the predicate elements are present. You can tell there are three exceptions to the prohibition in the rule. Each of the exceptions contains several elements. In the first exception, the testimony must relate to something—an uncontested issue. In the second exception, the testimony must relate to something—the nature *and* the value of legal services rendered in the case in which the lawyer is testifying. The third exception refers to the disqualification of the lawyer to be his client's advocate in the case covered by the general prohibition. That disqualification must do something—work substantial hardship.

Why is this important? Because one of the easiest ways, perhaps the single easiest way, for a lawyer to go astray at the outset of legal analysis is to overlook elements of the potentially relevant legal rules. Time and again, beginning legal thinkers and writers miss valuable lines of analysis because they do not make the threshold effort to break apart (and we mean *really* break apart) all (and we mean *every single one*) of the components of the legal standards. Read meticulously. Do not skip over language. Do not be misled by someone else's organization of the material, when that organization is not as finely parsed as yours. And as you evaluate the elements, think about the public policy explanations for the existence of the elements.

In the case of Minnesota Rule 3.7, for example, assume you represent a trust created by a now deceased member of a family. Over the last twenty years, you have been the lawyer who has given advice to the trustee who administers that trust, and you have represented the trustee in court six different times on issues relating to the interpretation of the document creating the trust. From time to time, you also have given personal legal advice to family members who are beneficiaries of the trust. That legal advice has been on matters unrelated to the trust. Now a dispute has arisen between the trustee and certain family members relating to interpretation of the trust document.

That dispute is about to go to trial (trial number 1). You expect to try the case in court. One of the family members is objecting to your participation as an advocate for the trustee, however, because you are expected to be a witness for that family member in the trial (trial number 2) of one of the unrelated matters on which you have given her legal advice in the past. How would you contest the objection?

You would analyze the question in the following way:

➢ Are you a lawyer? Yes.
➢ Do you plan to act as an advocate? Yes.
➢ At a trial? Yes, trial no. 1.
➢ In which you are likely to be a witness? No. You are going to be a witness in a different proceeding, trial no. 2.
➢ The rule does not apply to your circumstances.

Does that make sense from a public policy standpoint? Yes. One purpose of the rule is to preserve the integrity of proceedings by not having lawyers appear before a judge and/or jury simultaneously as advocates and as sources of facts. Another purpose is to avoid conflicts among lawyers and clients when the lawyers must zealously advocate cases at the same time that, as witnesses, they are sworn to tell the truth as to facts that might hurt the clients. When a lawyer is not acting as an advocate in the same trial as she is acting as a material witness, then the policy reasons behind the rule are not violated (although there still may be an unhappy client). So the lawyer can feel reasonably comfortable that her logic in parsing the rule is correct.

Two frequent questions are: First, may I now stop? The answer is no. Second, do I have to break apart all of the elements if I already think one is controlling in my problem? The answer is yes. Just because one element of the rule jumps out at you does not mean that you should avoid accounting for the others. You may gain new insights in accounting for all the elements. If you conclude that you may indeed forego additional consideration of some of the elements in your circumstances (because everyone concedes they are irrelevant, for example), then there is no harm done. You note their irrelevance and quickly move on. But you should train yourself to go through them in any event.

So in the Rule 3.7 problem, keep going through the elements even though you think there is a dispositive argument that the rule simply does not apply. Assume, hypothetically, that trial number 1 and trial number 2 were going to be the same, single trial. *Even if* you were going to be a witness in that trial, are you likely to be a necessary witness? The answer is unclear on the known facts. *Even if* you were likely to be a necessary witness in that trial, might you be testifying on an uncontested issue? The answer is unclear on the known facts. *Even if* you were likely to be a necessary witness in that trial, might you be testifying about the nature and value of the services you rendered? The answer is unclear on the known facts. *Even if* you were likely to be a necessary witness in that trial, might your disqualification as trial counsel work substantial hardship on the trustee for the trust? The answer is likely yes. You have been the trust's counsel for twenty years, as well as its advocate in court six previous times on matters of trust interpretation. The rule seeks to preserve the integrity of court proceedings and to avoid placing lawyers in potential conflict situations with clients; but the rule also seeks to preserve a client's choice of counsel, to avoid hardship. What should you do? You now may assert a second, subsidiary argument against the objection to your serving as advocate: *Even if* trial number 1 and trial number 2 *were* the same, the family member's objection should still be denied because your disqualification would work substantial hardship on the trustee within the meaning of the "unless" clause (3).

Working through all of the elements of Rule 3.7 thus has enabled you to adopt a classic two-pronged analysis of the relevant rule: First, the family member's objection should be denied because Rule 3.7(a) does not apply, i.e., you are not going to be a witness in the same trial in which you are acting as an advocate. Second, even if Rule 3.7(a) did apply, your disqualification as counsel would work a substantial hardship on the trustee, and thus the court should reject the disqualification attempt.[2]

---

[2] You may be able to construct additional arguments by digging for more facts relating to the questions whose answers are currently unclear.

Note, of course, that there may be debate about how courts have applied such terms in the rule as "substantial hardship." Like the word "reasonable," which was discussed in Chapter 3, determining what is a "substantial hardship" likely will involve a fact-specific analysis, i.e., comparing and contrasting the facts of your case to those of other cases in which courts have applied the term.

COMMON MISTAKES IN PARSING A RULE

There are a number of mistakes that beginners tend to make in parsing rules.

Common Mistake No. 1: Sloppy Reading

It is easy for a reader in a hurry to run through a rule too quickly and thereby miss components or important structural features. Consider Rule 3.7(a), for example. The word "unless" modifies all three of the exceptions, which are "either/or" clauses. When you construct your outline of Rule 3.7(a), do not associate the word "unless" only with the very first exception. Similarly, do not treat the three exceptions as cumulative instead of alternative.

Common Mistake No. 2: Imprecise Paraphrasing

Be careful when paraphrasing the language of rules for your own interpretation or when you are explaining the rule in writing. For example, suppose in Rule 3.7(a) that you substituted the word "proceeding" for the word "trial." That paraphrase may have actually changed the meaning of the rule. "Proceeding" may well be a broader term than "trial." Your change of words may actually cause you to give mistaken advice. When in doubt, do not paraphrase. And never substitute a paraphrased identification of a rule for the actual text. In other words, always begin your analysis with the actual text of the rule. Only then is it permissible to paraphrase the text in explaining the rule.

Common Mistake No. 3:
Converting Negative Language into Positive

It is tempting to convert "shall not" negatively phrased rules into "may" positively phrased rules. From the standpoint of language flow, this conversion is appealing. But watch out! Conversions can be dangerous, because they can be tricky to accomplish without accidentally changing the rule. For example, you might think about changing Rule 3.7(a) from a "shall not" structure to a "may" structure: "A lawyer MAY act as advocate at a trial in which the lawyer is likely to be a necessary witness WHEN . . . ." Notice three things about what this does: First, each of the three exceptions to the "shall not" rule now becomes a predicate for the "may" rule. Second, you happen to be lucky: the conversion process with Rule 3.7(a) can be accomplished without changing an explicit or implicit "or" clause to an "and" clause. The conversion can also be accomplished without inserting the word "not" into the three-exception/predicate clauses. But do not assume this is always conveniently true. Third, you have created a new and different bottom line standard: In the original rule, the assumption is that there are only three circumstances when a lawyer can both testify and advocate in the same trial. In the new converted rule, the assumption is that the lawyer may both testify and advocate in the same trial under each of three circumstances, but do you actually know what the lawyer should do in other circumstances? The answer is probably no, you do not know what the lawyer should do. So do you have to add the word "ONLY" in front of the word "WHEN," to make the meaning of the rule clearer? That kind of additional conversion can be easy to forget, which is why conversions are dangerous.

Common Mistake No. 4:
Assuming Your Detailed Outline of the Rule
Elements Is for Public Consumption

Your detailed outline for breaking apart a rule is for your own use, to help you make sure that you are not overlooking material components of the rule that might bear on the answer to the legal problem you have to solve. The outline is not what you typically will provide a court, a client, a colleague, or other audiences. When you prepare a rule analysis for persons other than yourself, you will begin with the actual text, but you will then be able to cluster the components, because some will be irrelevant or undisputed for purposes of the problem you are solving. The focus for now, however, is on your own personal understanding of the nuances of the rule bearing upon your problem. So err on the side of making your outline of the material elements of the rule as detailed as possible for your own use.

Common Mistake No. 5:
Assuming You Never Have to Consult Case Law, or
That You Always Must Consult Case Law

Recall that Minnesota Rule 3.7 included a term, "substantial hardship," that likely requires looking to case law to determine which facts have risen to the level of "substantial hardship," and which have not. Sometimes it will be clear that a legislature, for example, intended to leave the detailed meaning of an enacted provision to the decision of the courts in light of the courts' reason and experience. In this situation, the problem solver must synthesize a series of cases where courts have applied the language, even in a threshold effort to understand what the words likely mean. This is accomplished by looking at the spectrum of case authority (using the techniques for reading cases described in Chapters 4, 5, and 6) and using a compare and contrast form of analysis, which is discussed in additional depth in Chapter 11.

Alternatively, there will be times when the language of an enacted provision of law is clear on its face. In that setting, a review of court decisions will initially be less important. As is typical in legal settings, therefore, "never" and "always" can be dangerous mind-sets. As you gain experience, you will be able to ascertain when a statutory term requires no additional research and when it does.

ASSEMBLING A RULE FROM A
SINGLE COURT DECISION

In the Minnesota Rule 3.7 example, we gave you the rule and asked you to break it apart. But what if you are not given a rule? What if you have to figure out what the rule is, before you can begin disassembling it to apply it to resolve a legal issue? This is a typical problem when working with court decisions as opposed to enacted law, model rules, codes, and the like. We will start with the simplest version of the task—assembly of a rule from the language in a single court decision.

Assume that you are a lawyer for a gigantic company in the pharmaceutical industry. Your client wants to sue a competitor for theft of a trade secret, namely the chemical formula for a prototype of a drug that will cure a dreaded disease. The competitor likely will counterclaim that the lawsuit is predatory, designed simply to distract the competitor from its efforts to develop its own similar drug and to maintain your client's dominant position in the industry. The evidence in your possession indicates that your client put elaborate security precautions into place to protect the relevant formula, but that the competitor nonetheless was able to obtain the details from a disgruntled former employee of your client's research department, who violated the confidentiality provision in his employment agreement. You also know that your client is locked in a desperate race with the competitor to be the first company to bring the relevant drug to market, and the client's files are replete with minutes of brainstorming sessions in which your client's employees have discussed how to impede the competitor's efforts. The client wants your advice as to the viability of the likely counterclaim.

You find the United States Supreme Court opinion in *Professional Real Estate Investors v. Columbia Pictures*, 508 U.S. 49, 113 S. Ct. 1920 (1993). You already know the following basic information: The federal antitrust laws regulate the competitive process in the United States. One of those laws is the Sherman Act, 15. U.S.C. § 1 *et seq*. Section 1 of the Act prohibits contracts, combinations, and conspiracies in (unreasonable) restraint of trade.[3] Section 2 of the Act prohibits monopolization, attempts to monopolize, and conspiracies to monopolize.[4] At the same time, the United States Constitution, through the Bill of Rights, preserves the right of the people to petition the government, and the Sherman Act is meant to regulate business activity, not political activity.[5] The courts are considered part of the "government."[6] So, a genuine effort to obtain law enforcement through a

---

[3] *E.g. Bd. of Trade of City of Chi. v. U.S.*, 246 U.S. 231, 38 S. Ct. 242 (1918).

[4] *E.g. Spectrum Sports, Inc. v. McQuillan*, 506 U.S. 447, 113 S. Ct. 884 (1993).

[5] *E.g. E. R.R. Pres. Conf. v. Noerr Motor Freight Co.*, 365 U.S. 127, 81 S. Ct. 523 (1961).

[6] *E.g. Cal. Motor Transport Co. v. Trucking Unlimited*, 404 U.S. 508, 92 S. Ct. 609 (1972).

lawsuit filed in court cannot be a Sherman Act violation.[7] But what if the lawsuit is just a "sham," a disguised effort simply to hurt a competitor? That is the question that *Professional Real Estate Investors* addresses.

Read the majority opinion excerpts below (from which we have omitted footnotes, a number of citations, and other materials for the sake of brevity).[8] See if you can describe the "rule" from the case before we talk about it.

Professional Real Estate Investors, Inc. v. Columbia Pictures
508 U.S. 49, 113 S. Ct. 1920 (1993)

This case requires us to define the "sham" exception to the doctrine of antitrust immunity first identified in *Eastern R. Presidents Conference v. Noerr Motor Freight, Inc.*, 365 U.S. 127 (1961), as the doctrine applies in the litigation context. . . . We hold that litigation cannot be deprived of immunity as a sham unless the litigation is objectively baseless. The Court of Appeals for the Ninth Circuit refused to characterize as sham a lawsuit that the antitrust defendant admittedly had probable cause to institute. We affirm.

I

Petitioners Professional Real Estate Investors, Inc., and Kenneth F. Irwin (collectively, PRE) operated la Mancha Private Club and Villas, a resort hotel in Palm Springs, California. Having installed videodisc players in the resort's hotel rooms and assembled a library of more than 200 motion picture titles, PRE rented videodiscs to guests for in-room viewing. PRE also sought to develop a market for the sale of videodisc players to other hotels wishing to offer in-room viewing of prerecorded material. Respondents, Columbia Pictures Industries, Inc., and seven other major motion picture studios (collectively, Columbia) held copyrights to the motion pictures recorded on the videodiscs that PRE purchased. Columbia also licensed the transmission of copyrighted motion pictures to hotel rooms through a wired cable system called Spectradyne. PRE therefore competed with Columbia not only for the viewing market at La Mancha but also for the broader market for in-room entertainment services in hotels.

---

[7] *E.g. MCI Commun. Corp. v. AT&T Co.*, 708 F.2d 1081 (7th Cir. 1983).

[8] For present purposes, we have chosen to use ellipses to denote all omissions. We note, however, that some citation rules require special treatment for omitting footnotes and citations from opinions.

In 1983, Columbia sued PRE for alleged copyright infringement through the rental of videodiscs for viewing in hotel rooms. PRE counter-claimed, charging Columbia with violations of §§ 1 and 2 of the Sherman Act . . . . In particular, PRE alleged that Columbia's copyright action was a mere sham that cloaked underlying acts of monopolization and conspiracy to restrain trade.

The parties filed cross-motions for summary judgment on Columbia's copyright claim and postponed further discovery on PRE's antitrust counterclaims. Columbia did not dispute that PRE could freely sell or lease lawfully purchased videodiscs under the Copyright Act's "first sale" doctrine, . . . and PRE conceded that the playing of videodiscs constituted "performance" of motion pictures . . . . As a result, summary judgment depended solely on whether rental of videodiscs for in-room viewing infringed Columbia's exclusive right to "perform the copyrighted work[s] publicly." . . . Ruling that such rental did not constitute public performance, the District Court entered summary judgment for PRE. . . . The Court of Appeals affirmed on the grounds that a hotel room was not a "public place" and that PRE did not "transmit or otherwise communicate" Columbia's motion pictures. . .

On remand, Columbia sought summary judgment on PRE's antitrust claims, arguing that the original copyright infringement action was no sham and was therefore entitled to immunity under *Eastern R. Presidents Conference v. Noerr Motor Freight, Inc., supra.* Reasoning that the infringement action "was clearly a legitimate effort and therefore not a sham,". . . the District Court granted the motion . . . .

· · ·

II

· · ·

In *California Motor Transport Co. v. Trucking Unlimited*, 404 U.S. 508 (1972), we elaborated on *Noerr* in two relevant respects. . . . We left unresolved the question presented by this case—whether litigation may be sham merely because a subjective expectation of success does not motivate the litigant. We now answer this question in the negative and hold that an objectively reasonable effort to litigate cannot be sham regardless of subjective intent.

· · ·

. . . Our recognition of a sham in [*California Motor Transport*] signifies that the institution of legal proceedings "without probable cause" will give rise to a sham if such activity effectively "bar[s] . . . competitors from meaningful access to adjudicatory tribunals and so . . . usurp[s] th[e] decision making process."

.   .   .

III

We now outline a two-part definition of "sham" litigation. First, the lawsuit must be objectively baseless in the sense that no reasonable litigant could realistically expect success on the merits. If an objective litigant could conclude that the suit is reasonably calculated to elicit a favorable outcome, the suit is immunized under *Noerr,* and an antitrust claim premised on the sham exception must fail. Only if challenged litigation is objectively meritless may a court examine the litigant's subjective motivation. Under this second part of our definition of sham, the court should focus on whether the baseless lawsuit conceals "an attempt to interfere *directly* with the business relationships of a competitor," . . . through the "use [of] the governmental *process*—as opposed to the *outcome* of that process—as an anticompetitive weapon," . . . . This two-tiered process requires the plaintiff to disprove the challenged lawsuit's *legal* viability before the court will entertain evidence of the suit's *economic* viability. . . .

.   .   .

IV

.   .   .

The existence of probable cause to institute legal proceedings precludes a finding that an antitrust defendant has engaged in sham litigation. The notion of probable cause, as understood and applied in the common law tort of wrongful civil proceedings, requires the plaintiff to prove that the defendant lacked probable cause to institute an unsuccessful civil lawsuit and that the defendant pressed the action for an improper, malicious purpose. . . . Probable cause to institute civil proceedings requires no more than a 'reasonabl[e] belie[f] that there is a chance that [a] claim may be held valid upon adjudication." . . . Because the absence of probable cause is an essential element of the tort, the existence of probable cause is an absolute defense . . . . Under our decision today, therefore, a proper probable cause determination irrefutably demonstrates that an antitrust plaintiff has not proved the objective prong of the sham exception and that the defendant is accordingly entitled to *Noerr* immunity.

The District Court and the Court of Appeals correctly found that Columbia had probable cause to sue PRE for copyright infringement.

What is the rule announced in *Professional Real Estate Investors*? You actually have several different possibilities. In the opening paragraph of the excerpted majority opinion, the Court stated that "[w]e hold that litigation cannot be deprived of immunity as a sham unless the litigation is objectively baseless." But then the Court also stated that "[w]e . . . hold that an objectively reasonable effort to litigate cannot be sham regardless of subjective intent." Are the concepts of "[not] objectively baseless" and "objectively reasonable" the same? They both purport to be "holdings" of the Court.

And what are the roles of two other parts of the opinion—the two-part definition of sham litigation and the discussion of probable cause? In the two-part definition, the Court explained that, to be a sham, a "lawsuit must be objectively baseless in the sense that no reasonable litigant could realistically expect success on the merits." Then, *if* the lawsuit is objectively baseless, it may be a sham when the litigant's subjective motive is *additionally* anticompetitive (as when the litigant intends the lawsuit itself to interfere with a competitor's business regardless of the ultimate outcome of the case). Is the two-part definition designed to explain what "objectively baseless" means, or what "objectively reasonable" means, or both? And what if a litigant files a lawsuit against a competitor, knowing that (a) the litigant has a fair chance of winning on the merits; (b) the costs of the litigation will outweigh the value of the victory; but (c) the litigant will inflict severe litigation costs, regardless of outcome, on the competitor who has fewer financial resources? Under the definition in *Professional Real Estate Investors*, is that "sham litigation"?[9]

What about the "probable cause" discussion? The Court wrote that "[t]he existence of probable cause to institute legal proceedings precludes a finding that an antitrust defendant has engaged in sham litigation." Is that simply a second way of characterizing the two-part definition of sham litigation? Or is it really an alternative test?

---

[9] If you were actually giving client advice, you would read the concurring opinion of Justice Stevens (not reprinted here) for additional insight.

There are really no perfect answers to the above questions.[10] Assuming multiple choices exist for assembling a rule from a court opinion, however, you would pursue the following six steps:

Step 1: Look for the words, "we hold that . . . ." These words may signal the announcement of the legal rule in the case, although they may instead simply signal the announcement of the outcome rather than the legal principle adopted by the court. So watch out. There are two "we hold that" statements in *Professional Real Estate Investors*, and one reasonable formulation of the legal rule from the case would involve combining the two statements—i.e., "litigation is not 'sham' if the litigation is objectively reasonable on its merits without regard to the subjective motivations of the person filing the suit."

Step 2: Look for the result in the case. Whatever the rule is, it must be consistent with, as well as explain, the result. For example, suppose you read a court opinion and tentatively conclude that the relevant rule in the case is composed of four elements. You then look at the result in the case and read that the plaintiff has won. You then look back at the facts in the case and notice that, given the facts, plaintiff could not have prevailed if element 3 in your proposed four-part rule is actually part of the equation. By definition, assuming that you have correctly identified the result and the material facts from the case, your proposed formulation of the rule must be incorrect, at least as to proposed element 3.

In *Professional Real Estate Investors*, you might conclude that the winner (Columbia Pictures) won because it had reasonable cause to believe that Professional Real Estate Investors was violating Columbia's copyright on movies. Thus, you might formulate the relevant legal rule as being that "litigation is not 'sham' if the person filing the litigation has reasonable cause to believe that the sued party is violating the legal right that the person seeks

---

[10] The fact that we are even asking the questions illustrates the helpfulness to your audience of saying something once, and not re-characterizing it multiple times unless you absolutely have to do so. Sometimes re-characterization language can be explained by the existence of multiple persons who must sign off on the text of a document before it is issued. Also, sometimes re-characterization language can be explained by the need to reconcile your writing with the approach taken by a previous writer (as in the case of an appellate court reviewing a lower court's decision in the same case). But still strive to say what you mean once clearly, and then get out.

to enforce in the litigation." You would not formulate the rule as being that "litigation may be sham when a subjective expectation of success does not motivate the litigant," because there is no indication that Columbia could have prevailed on summary judgment if subjective intent alone were the rule.

Step 3: In selecting or formulating the succinct explanation, start with the narrowest statement that fully explains the resolution of the problem the court addressed. The true legal rule of the case does not include any statements about the law that are unnecessary to the resolution of the problem before the court. By the same token, your succinct explanation of the rule of the case is _too_ succinct if you cannot fully explain the outcome from it.

In _Professional Real Estate Investors_, you might conclude that much of the language in the majority opinion is unnecessary. You might conclude that much of the language is not the narrowest statement that fully explains the resolution of the problem the court addressed. You might conclude that the second part of the Court's two-part test (the subjective motivation part of the objective reasonableness/subjective motivation standard) for analyzing a "sham" lawsuit was irrelevant to the facts at hand in the case. Columbia Pictures had a reasonable chance of winning its copyright claim on the merits, even if ultimately it did not prevail on that claim. Whether Columbia was subjectively motivated by a desire to hurt Professional Real Estate Investors competitively was ultimately irrelevant. Thus, you might conclude that the legal rule in the case should resemble the one in Step 2 "look for the result" discussion above, but not the rule formulated in Step 1 "we hold that" discussion.

Step 4: If there appear to be multiple, appropriate formulations of the legal rule in the case after you apply the three previous steps, then put all of the potential formulations side-by-side and do two things: First, look for elements of the rule that are common to more than one of the formulations. You can be reasonably sure that common elements are part of the court's definition of the relevant rule. Second, in choosing among multiple, appropriate formulations, opt for the version that is most helpful to your preferred resolution of the problem in your own case.

Applying Step 4 to _Professional Real Estate Investors_, you might put "[not] objectively baseless," "objectively reasonable," and "having probable cause" side-by-side and notice that the word "objectively" appears more than once and is thus likely part of the relevant definition of "good faith." You might also conclude hypothetically that "[not] objectively baseless" and "objectively reasonable" are equally viable legal definitions of a lawsuit that is not a "sham," in which case you should pick the one that favors your own circumstances.

Step 5: Go back and compare the results you obtain from all four of the above steps to try to ensure that your selected rule formulation is consistent with the thrust of the court's opinion. It is perilous to zero in on a snippet of language in a court's opinion as being the rule in the case if your selection of language appears inconsistent with the outcome, or inconsistent with the majority of the rules produced by your efforts under Steps 1 through 4 above.

Step 6: Consider the policy implications of your rule formulation, and ask yourself if your construction of the rule is consistent with the policies that the court expressly or impliedly is seeking to uphold. In the *Professional Real Estate Investors* opinion, the Court was seeking to balance two competing considerations. On the one hand, the Court wanted to make sure that litigants are free to exercise their right to seek relief in court for perceived legal violations. Otherwise, the system would encourage people to engage simply in self-help to remedy perceived wrongs. On the other hand, the court system should not be a pawn for misuse by businesses. So the Court sought to formulate a quasi-objective test for differentiating between genuine and "sham" lawsuits.

Template for assembling a rule from a case:

➤ Look for the words, "we hold that . . . ."
➤ Look for the result in the case.
➤ Look for the narrowest statement that explains the resolution.
➤ Compare the potential formulations side-by-side.
➤ Look for the thrust of the court's opinion.
➤ Consider the policy implications.

So what advice would you give your client in our hypothetical pharmaceutical problem? If the formula for the proprietary drug has indeed been well guarded, and the competitor has indeed stolen the formula by causing a former employee of your client to divulge the secret formula in violation of a confidentiality agreement, then your client's proposed lawsuit against the competitor appears to have an objectively reasonable basis. If it does, then your client's interest in slowing down the competitor is ultimately irrelevant. Under *Professional Real Estate Investors*, an antitrust counterclaim likely should fail.

CHAPTER 5

Determining the Rule
in Typical, Complex Scenarios

What if there are multiple court decisions from which you must assemble a rule? Now the rule assembly is becoming more complex. You have to reconcile different cases that discuss the same basic legal concept and make sense out of the language.

ASSEMBLING A RULE FROM MULTIPLE COURT DECISIONS

Assume that your client, a real estate agency, presents you with the following problem. The client wishes to recruit and hire a sales agent who works for a competing company. The agent has a contract with the competitor that allows either the agent or the competitor to terminate the contract at will on thirty days notice. The client has heard that the competitor is aggressive about retaining its sales agents and looks for excuses to sue real estate agencies that try to hire away the agents. The client wants your advice as to the likelihood of a legitimate claim.

Read the four excerpts below (from which we have omitted footnotes, a number of citations, and other materials for the sake of brevity). See if you can describe the rule from the cases before we discuss them.

RJM Sales & Marketing, Inc. v. Banfi Products Corp.
546 F. Supp. 1368 (D. Minn. 1982)

[Authors' note: Defendant Banfi Products Corp. ("Banfi") was a manufacturer of beverages and an importer of wines. RJM Sales & Marketing, Inc. ("RJM") was a broker for beverage manufacturers. Banfi contracted with RJM to be a broker of Banfi's products. The contract included a termination clause, which stated: "Either party to this agreement may terminate it by giving thirty (30) days written notice to the other party." Fifteen months after contracting with RJM, Banfi terminated the agreement. Shortly after that, Banfi hired a former employee of RJM to become Banfi's broker. That employee, Howard Mourer, had tendered his resignation at RJM on April 6, 1981, effective on May 1, 1981, and was hired by Banfi on May 1. These events caused RJM to sue Banfi on a number of causes of action, which included a claim that Banfi tortiously interfered with Mourer's employment at RJM by hiring him away.]

Counts 9 and 10 of RJM's amended complaint are based on Banfi's alleged hiring away of Howard Mourer, RJM's employee for North and South Dakota, to be Banfi's broker for those states. RJM alleges that Banfi tortiously interfered with RJM's contract with Mourer by procuring Mourer's resignation, and that this activity constituted unfair competition.

Mourer's employment contract with RJM was terminable at will. The prevailing rule in Minnesota and elsewhere is that one is not liable for interfering with the rights of parties to a contract that is terminable at will. . . . In some jurisdictions a cause of action nevertheless exists "if either the defecting employee or the competitor . . . is guilty of some concomitant, unconscionable conduct . . . ," . . . such as misappropriation of trade secrets, . . . enticing away the employer's customers, . . . or intending to cripple the employer's business . . . .

Counsel for RJM attempted to take advantage of this exception by arguing that Banfi's hiring of Mourer was part of a larger conspiracy or plot to terminate RJM. By hiring Mourer, counsel argued, Banfi would obtain a broker experienced in the North and South Dakota markets and be in a position to terminate its relationship with RJM. Even assuming that this was Banfi's purpose, Banfi's conduct can still not be considered "unconscionable" since, under the contract, Banfi had the right to terminate RJM as its broker at any time upon 30 days notice.

. . . The Court concludes that RJM has no cause of action under Counts 9 and 10 of its complaint.

Hough Transit, Ltd. v. National Farmers Organization
472 N.W.2d 358 (Minn. App. 1991)

[Authors' note: Hough Transit, Ltd. ("Hough") was a trucking service hauling milk from farmers to creameries. National Farmers Organization ("the co-op") was a farmer cooperative. The cooperative had a practice of using Hough to transport its milk. In 1988, the cooperative became dissatisfied with Hough and approached one of Hough's truck drivers about the possibility of starting his own milk hauling business. The driver did so, taking over the co-op's milk routes. In subsequent litigation, Hough claimed, among other things, that the co-op had tortiously interfered with the relationship between Hough and its former driver.]

[T]he co-op cannot be liable in tort for interfering with the rights of the driver and Hough because their contract was terminable at-will. . . . Even if Minnesota were to recognize a cause of action for tortious interference with an at-will relationship, there is no evidence the co-op improperly enticed the driver away from Hough's employment. Instead, the record shows the co-op members simply asked the driver to haul the co-op routes and the driver agreed. This job offer did not rise to the level of an improper interference with Hough's relationship with the driver. . . . Under these circumstances, the trial court properly granted summary judgment [for the co-op].

Oak Park Development Co., Inc. v. Snyder Brothers of Minnesota, Inc.
499 N.W.2d 500 (Minn. App. 1993)

[Authors' note: Oak Park Development Co., Inc. ("Oak Park") owned the St. Croix shopping mall. Snyder Brothers of Minnesota, Inc. ("Snyder Brothers") was a tenant in the mall. The lease agreement required Snyder Brothers to subordinate its lease to any mortgage on the property. In connection with a mall expansion that would involve adding a Herberger's store to the mall, Oak Park asked Snyder Brothers to sign a subordination agreement, expressly subordinating the Snyder lease to a mortgage that would secure financing for the Herberger store construction project. Snyder Brothers eventually produced the subordination agreement, but not before Herberger's decided to locate in another mall after the closing on the mortgage financing had to be delayed for lack of Snyder's subordination document. Oak Park then sued Snyder Brothers, alleging that Snyder Brothers unreasonably delayed signing the subordination agreement in order to extract concessions from Oak Park on Snyder's own lease, and that this tortiously interfered with Oak Park's prospective deal with Herberger's.]

The elements of interference with contract are: (1) the existence of a contract; (2) the alleged tortfeasor's knowledge of the contract; (3) the intentional interference with the contract; (4) without justification; and (5) damages resulting from the interference. . . .

.   .   .

Although the Oak Park/Herberger's lease was terminable at will, a binding contract was still in existence, and thus any interference was actionable. *See e.g. Michaelson v. Minnesota Mining & Mfg. Co.*, 474 N.W.2d 174, 180 (Minn. App. 1991), *aff'd*, 479 N.W.2d 58 (Minn. 1992). In *Michaelson*, this court stated: "A person may be held liable for interference with a contract, however, even if the contract is terminable at will." *Id.* at 181. . . .

We do agree, however, with the trial court's analysis that Snyder Brothers did not intentionally interfere with the Oak Park/Herberger's contract. There is no evidence that Snyder Brothers did anything to intentionally induce Herberger's to terminate its contract with Oak Park. Rather, Herberger's simply terminated its contract with Oak Park after receiving a superior offer from [the other mall].

Many of the delays in this case resulted from Oak Park's actions or inaction. . . . In light of all the facts, it is not plausible to presume the Herberger's store was not built due solely to Snyder Brother's delay in delivering the subordination agreement. . . .

.   .   .

The trial court did not err in granting summary judgment for Snyder Brothers . . . .

J.N.R. Enterprises, Inc. v. Frigidaire Co.
1999 WL 377747 (Minn. App. 1999) (Unpublished Opinion)

[Authors' note: J.N.R. Enterprises ("JNR") was a distributor of Frigidaire Company ("Frigidaire") appliances to commercial users. In early 1997, JNR and Frigidaire entered into an agreement requiring JNR to maintain an adequate sales and service staff, as well as to maintain suitable office and warehousing facilities. In late 1997, Frigidaire terminated JNR as a distributor. Frigidaire cited JNR's alleged failure to comply with the distribution agreement. JNR in turn commenced a lawsuit against Frigidaire and ALL, Inc. ("ALL"), one of JNR's competitors. JNR alleged, among other things, that ALL wrongfully procured the termination, through tortious interference with JNR's relationship with Frigidaire. JNR further alleged that ALL accomplished the interference, at least in part, by defaming JNR because ALL falsely had told Frigidaire employees that JNR was not fulfilling its contract obligations to Frigidaire. The district court granted summary judgment to ALL on the tortious interference claim (and a separate defamation claim), and JNR appealed.]

A cause of action for wrongful interference with a contractual relationship requires (1) a contract, (2) knowledge of that contract by the wrongdoer, (3) intentional interference with the contract, (4) without justification, and (5) damages. . . . To establish the third element of the cause of action, a plaintiff may show that the defendant induced a third party to breach the contract or that the defendant intentionally interfered with the plaintiff's contractual rights by committing an independent tort. . . . A party may be held liable for interference with a contract even if the contract is terminable at will. . . .

. . . This court has held that interference with a binding contract terminable at will is actionable, even if the contract is not breached. . . .

Because JNR alleged no other independent tort, the only tort upon which JNR can base its tortious interference claim is defamation. . . . JNR's defamation claim was not properly dismissed on summary judgment. Accordingly, the defamation claim may properly serve as a basis for JNR's tortious interference with contractual relations claim. . . . For the foregoing reasons, the district court erred in granting summary judgment dismissing JNR's tortious interference claim.

How would you describe Minnesota's tortious-interference-with-contract rule if the above four cases were the only ones you had available? The following template is one possible way of approaching the assembly of the relevant rule.

Step 1: Start by identifying the most recent, most authoritative case. Let's examine the available possibilities. The *RJM* decision is the oldest of the four cases (1982) and, in addition, is a federal court opinion. Federal courts may use state legal rules to resolve problems in cases properly before them, but federal courts do not authoritatively make state law.

The *Hough Transit* decision is more recent (1991), and it is a published decision of the Minnesota Court of Appeals. In the absence of a Minnesota Supreme Court opinion in our hypothetical group of only four opinions, the Minnesota Court of Appeals is the most authoritative court in the pool. But there are two more recent opinions from the same court available to us, so *Hough Transit* is not the most recent, most authoritative case.

The *Oak Park Development* decision (1993) is a later case from the court of appeals, and it is published. The *J.N.R* decision (1999) is the most recent case from the court of appeals, but it is not published. Minnesota Statute 480A.08, subdivision 3(b), provides that "[u]npublished opinions of the court of appeals are not precedential." Thus, the most recent, most authoritative decision is *Oak Park Development*.[1]

Step 2: Determine what the most recent, most authoritative decision says the relevant legal rule is (using the six-step process from the "assembling a rule from a single court decision" discussion in Chapter 4), and look at the result in the case. The *Oak Park Development* court stated three key things about tortious interference with contract that produced a victory for Snyder Brothers. First, the "elements of interference with contract are: (1) the existence of a contract; (2) the alleged tortfeasor's knowledge of the contract; (3) the intentional interference with the contract; (4) without justification; and (5) damages resulting from the interference." Second, there can be tortious interference with a terminable-at-will contract. These appear to be statements of legal rules. Third, the court explained the definition of "intentional" by stating that Snyder Brothers did nothing to procure Herberger's move to a different mall. Note that and tuck it away for possible further use.

Step 3: Ask yourself how the selected authoritative court's statement of the rule squares with the statements and the results in the other available cases. Let's turn to the other three decisions in our pool. *RJM* is the early federal court decision. It held that there is no such thing as tortious interference with a terminable-at-will contract. That does not appear to be a current statement of the law, however, because subsequent Minnesota appellate decisions (*Oak Park Development* and *J.N.R.*) hold otherwise. *RJM* may thus be discounted on the terminable-at-will point. The *RJM* court did, however, offer an aside that a cause of action might exist in some jurisdictions

---

[1] In Minnesota, although unpublished opinions are not precedential, they may nonetheless be cited by lawyers, provided the lawyers in a litigation context give copies to the relevant court and other counsel. Moreover, the reasoning in the opinions may be deemed persuasive and adopted. *Ge Lee v. Hunt,* 642 N.W.2d 57 (Minn. App. 2002). This will become relevant to our rule formulation steps at a later point down the line. You should always look at the procedural rules in your own jurisdiction to determine what use, if any, you may make of unpublished opinions. Different jurisdictions adopt different rules. In some courts, for example, unpublished court opinions are considered to have no precedential value and may not be cited.

if a defendant engages in "concomitant, unconscionable conduct," and it identified three examples: misappropriation of trade secrets, enticing away customers, and intending to cripple the plaintiff's business. Make a note of that and tuck it away to see if any similar concept shows up in the other cases. Notice also the result in *RJM*—the defendant won.

Hough Transit is the next case. The *Hough Transit* court stated there is no such thing as tortious interference with a terminable-at-will contract. *Hough Transit* does not appear to be a current statement of the law, given *Oak Park Development* and *J.N.R.* The *Hough Transit* decision thus can be discounted on the terminable-at-will point. It did, however, offer an aside that, even if Minnesota recognized a cause of action for tortious interference with a terminable-at-will contract, there would be no legal violation in *Hough Transit* because the co-op never did anything improper. All the co-op did was ask whether Hough Transit's truck driver would haul Hough Transit's routes. Make a note of that and tuck it away to see if any similar concept shows up in the other cases. Also notice the result in *Hough Transit*—the defendant won.

J.N.R. Enterprises is the last case. It postdates *Oak Park Development*. It is an unpublished case, but you know that, in Minnesota, unpublished opinions of the court of appeals may be cited (with proper notice), and their reasoning may even be persuasive and later adopted in published decisions. So it matters what *J.N.R.* holds.

What does the case hold? First, it stated that a cause of action for "wrongful interference with a contractual relationship requires (1) a contract, (2) knowledge of that contract by the wrongdoer, (3) intentional interference with the contract, (4) without justification, and (5) damages." This is almost identical language to *Oak Park Development*, and it gives us comfort that there are currently five elements to the cause of action. Second, the case stated that there can be tortious interference with a terminable-at-will contract. This is consistent with *Oak Park Development*, and it gives us comfort that contrary statements in *RJM* and in *Hough Transit* are no longer good law. Third, in commenting upon the "intentional interference" element of the cause of action, the *J.N.R.* court stated that a plaintiff may show that "the defendant induced a third party to breach the [relevant] contract, *or* that the defendant intentionally interfered with the plaintiff's contractual rights by *committing an independent tort*." (Emphasis added.) The court stated that the presence of the defamation claim in the case meant the plaintiff might go forward.

Can you now predict with some reasonable certainty what the rule of law is regarding the elements of a tortious-interference-with-contract claim, assuming the relevant universe of cases consists of the four with which we have been working? Yes. You can say with some confidence that there is such a cause of action that currently consists of five defined elements. The cause of action is likely available even in cases involving terminable-at-will contracts. You can predict with some confidence that a Minnesota court will permit an action to go forward, even in a case where the defendant technically does not procure an actual breach of a terminable-at-will contract, so long as the defendant's conduct is independently wrongful. Examples of such independently wrongful conduct likely include defamation and theft of trade secrets. In our one case where the cause of action did go forward, there was such alleged improper conduct (defamation). In our three cases where the defendant won, there was not.

Step 4: Test your conclusions against the reasoning of the authorities and common-sense policy considerations. Does our extraction of the relevant rules from the above cases make sense? Yes. In the rough-and-tumble commercial arena, all kinds of activities by competitors may "interfere" with existing contracts involving other players in business. If the courts called all of the interferences "tortious," the courts would be deluged with claims, and legitimate competition would be discouraged. What, then, do the courts really seek to prevent? They seek to prevent persons from inducing breaches of contract. They also seek to discourage independently wrongful conduct such as defamation and theft. The claim elements should mirror those concerns. In our formulation of the legal rules, they do.

Template for assembling a rule from multiple cases:

➢ Start with the most recent, most authoritative case.
➢ What does that case say the relevant legal rule is, and what result occurred?
➢ Square the rule and the result with the other cases.
➢ Test your conclusions against the reasoning of the authorities and common-sense policy considerations.

Some lawyers find it helpful to create a chart to reflect the analysis. This gives them a visual picture of the development of the law. Consider what a chart might look like in the abstract and then we will apply it to the tortious interference scenario in particular.

Two Sample Hypothetical Charts

Assume a matter that you will resolve by applying the law from four hypothetical precedents in a given state. Two of the precedents are state supreme court opinions from 1999 and 2004, respectively. The other two precedents are intermediate court of appeals opinions from 2002 and 2005, respectively. Assume that the opinions all discuss a legal rule containing three elements. You plot the opinions in a chart that looks something like the following:

	CASE 1	CASE 2	CASE 3	CASE 4
Court	State Supreme Court	State Court of Appeals	State Supreme Court	State Court of Appeals
Year	1999	2002	2004	2005
Result	Defendant wins	Defendant wins	Plaintiff wins	Defendant wins
Legal Rule	A claim for relief exists if: Element 1 Element 2 Element 3	A claim for relief exists if: Element 1 Element 2 Element 3	A claim for relief exists if: Element 1 Element 2 Element 3	A claim for relief exists if: Element 1 Element 2 Element 3
Facts	Facts favor the plaintiff on Elements 2 and 3, but not Element 1	Facts favor the plaintiff on Elements 1 and 3, but not Element 2	Facts favor the plaintiff on all of Elements 1, 2, and 3	Facts favor the plaintiff on Elements 1 and 2, but not Element 3

If you created such a chart to assist you in analyzing the case law precedents, what would you conclude? You would conclude that the legal rule to resolve your problem is well-settled—all of the four existing precedents identify and apply the same three-element legal test. You would also conclude that each of the three elements is a necessary part of the test—in the one case where the plaintiff won, the facts supported the plaintiff on each of the three elements of the test; on the other hand, in each and every other case where the plaintiff lost, the facts favored the defendant on one of the three elements. The logical conclusion is that the legal elements are connected by "ands." The plaintiff needs to prove Element 1 *and* Element 2 *and*

Element 3. The matrix is simple, and it provides a convenient picture of how the rule operates. At this point, you would go back and insert "*and*'s into the chart of the legal rule, if you had not already placed them in the outline.

Now, to give you a sense of how such a chart might be helpful in a more complex scenario, suppose a different set of five precedents. All of the precedents are state supreme court opinions. Each is from a different year. Assume that the opinions all discuss a legal rule containing three elements. You plot the opinions in a chart that looks something like this:

	CASE 1	CASE 2	CASE 3	CASE 4	CASE 5
Court	State Supreme Court	State Supreme Court	State Supreme Court	State Supreme Court	State Supreme Court
Year	1998	1999	2002	2004	2005
Result	Plaintiff wins	Plaintiff wins	Defendant wins	Plaintiff wins	Defendant wins
Legal Rule	A claim for relief exists if: Element 1 Element 2 Element 3	A claim for relief exists if: Element 1 Element 2 Element 3	A claim for relief exists if: Element 1 Element 2 Element 3	A claim for relief exists if: Element 1 Element 2 Element 3	A claim for relief exists if: Element 1 Element 2 Element 3
Facts	Facts favor the plaintiff on Elements 1, 2, and 3.	Facts favor the plaintiff on Elements 1 and 2. Facts favor the defendant on Element 3.	Facts favor the plaintiff on Elements 2 and 3. Facts favor the defendant on Element 1.	Facts favor the plaintiff on Elements 1 and 3. Facts favor the defendant on Element 2.	Facts favor the plaintiff on Element 1. Facts favor the defendant on Elements 2 and 3.

Using your chart, what would you conclude? All of the cases recite that the relevant legal rule contains three elements. So the "law" appears well-settled. And yet it looks as if not all of the elements have the same import.

Let's consider each element in turn. Element 1 is an important component of the rule. That element was discussed in all five cases. The facts favored the plaintiff on Element 1 in all three cases where the plaintiff won. And the only time the facts favored the defendant on Element 1, the defendant won the case even though both of Elements 2 and 3 favored the plaintiff. Element 1 is materially important to the results. Plaintiff must prove it to win.

Is winning on Element 1 sufficient by itself to produce an overall victory for the plaintiff? No. In every case in which plaintiff won, the facts also favored the plaintiff on at least one other additional element. Moreover, defendant won the case where the facts favored plaintiff on Element 1 but the facts favored the defendant on the other two elements.

What about Elements 2 and 3? They do appear to be part of the rule. They are discussed in all four cases. And plaintiff cannot win unless the facts favor plaintiff on at least one of those two elements. If defendant prevails on both of Elements 2 and 3, defendant wins.

So how do you explain what you see in the chart, for purposes of solving the client's problem? The legal rule appears to be a kind of balancing test. Element 1 is materially significant. Plaintiff needs to satisfy Element 1 to win. In addition, plaintiff needs one more of the two other elements, thereby prevailing on a majority of the three elements. You now need to insert an "*and*" after Element 1 in the chart, and then to indent the two other elements and insert an "or" between them, if you have not already placed the connectors in the outline.

Tortious Interference Cases Chart

How might a chart look in the tortious interference cases? One possibility follows:

	RJM Sales	*Hough*	*Oak Park*	*J.N.R. Enter.*
Court	D. Minn.	Minn. App.	Minn. App.	Minn. App.
Year	1982	1991	1993	1999
Result	Defendant Wins	Defendant Wins	Defendant Wins	Plaintiff wins (against summary judgment)
Legal Rule	No tort liability for interference with terminable at will contract. Hint: Possible liability for concomitant, unconscionable conduct.	No tort liability for interference with terminable at will contract. Hint: Possible liability for improper enticement.	A claim for relief exists if: 1. A contract 2. tortfeasor knowledge of contract 3. intentional interference 4. without justification 5. damages Possible claim if terminable at will contract.	A claim for relief exists if: 1. A contract 2. wrongdoer knowledge of contract 3. intentional interference 4. without justification 5. damages Possible claim if terminable at will contract. Claim if D. procures breach or commits independent tort.
Facts	D. hires away one of P.'s terminable at will employees. No bad conduct.	D. hires away one of P.'s terminable at will drivers. No improper conduct.	D. delays signing agreement. But not clear delay caused third-party to walk away from terminable at will lease with P.	D. mfr. terminates P. as distributor. Co-D. other distributor allegedly defames P. Causes termination? No breach of contract procured, but possible independent tort of defamation?

So now, what advice do you give your real estate client? Likely you state something along these lines: In theory, hiring away the competitor's sales agent could constitute "tortious interference" with contract under current law. The two latest cases recognize there may be interference with a terminable contract, and one of the cases allowed a claim by a plaintiff to proceed. However, because the agent's contract with the competitor is terminable at will by either party, the hiring of the agent does not procure a breach of the contract. When the hiring does not procure a breach of an existing contract, there is no tortious interference unless the hiring is accompanied by other wrongful conduct, such as theft of trade secrets. So if you hire the agent from the competitor, make sure that in the employment agreement and in practice you take visible steps to ensure that the agent does not reveal to you any information that the competitor might consider a trade secret, such as information about specific prospective clients or about proprietary computer systems.

COMMON MISTAKES IN ASSEMBLING A RULE FROM MULTIPLE CASES

There are a number of mistakes you should try to avoid making when assembling a rule from multiple cases.

Common Mistake No. 1:
Assuming that a Legal Rule Is Consistent
Across Multiple Cases

Look for subtle (and sometimes not-so-subtle) additions to and subtractions from legal rules—even where courts say nothing expressly about those. It is important to take the multiple cases, place them side-by-side, and compare their facts, their rule statements, and their results. If the winner in case number 2 could not have won under the elements of the rule announced in case number 1, then the rules in the two cases *are* different, whether the courts have bothered to say so or not.

Common Mistake No. 2:
Failing to Focus on the Dates of Decisions

In general, recent authority trumps older authority. But note that pairing an older decision with a recent decision can be an effective way to demonstrate the continued vitality of a long-standing, venerable rule.

Common Mistake No. 3:
Failing to Focus on Court Hierarchy

In general, supreme court authority trumps intermediate appellate court authority, which in turn trumps trial court authority.[2]

Common Mistake No. 4:
Failing to Focus on Binding Authority

Recall from Chapter 3 that the decisions of the courts in your specific jurisdiction are mandatory authority. The decisions of the courts in other jurisdictions are merely persuasive. If the question you are analyzing is a matter of state law, the decisions of the state courts in that state are binding. If the question you are analyzing is a matter of federal law, the decisions of the United States Supreme Court, federal court of appeals for your circuit, and the federal district court in your district are binding. You cannot ignore binding authority merely because you like a particular persuasive authority better.[3]

---

[2] The terminology can be confusing. In New York, for example, the name of the highest court is the New York Court of Appeals. New York Supreme Court, General Term, is actually the name given to trial courts. So you simply have to become familiar with the terminology in the specific jurisdiction whose law you are analyzing.

[3] Note that the question of mandatory versus persuasive authority can become quite complex in various circumstances. For example, assume that a client wants you to analyze a Minnesota contract. You find a Minnesota Supreme Court case involving similar facts that applied Michigan contract law to an agreement between a Minnesota resident and a Michigan resident. Is the Minnesota Supreme Court decision mandatory authority for your problem? Not really, in the sense that, although the question involved a matter of state law, and the Minnesota Supreme Court is the highest court in the state, the decision applied Michigan law, and is thus merely persuasive authority for your problem.

CHAPTER 6

Determining the Rule
in Atypical Scenarios

An even more difficult rule assembly process occurs when there are directly conflicting cases in a particular jurisdiction, or when you are faced with a case of first impression (i.e., your jurisdiction has not addressed the particular legal problem before).

ASSEMBLING RULES IN ATYPICAL SETTINGS: DIRECT CONFLICTS

Assume that in our prior "tortious interference" discussion, you found only two Minnesota cases on point. One was the *Hough Transit* decision, decided on June 25, 1991, and the other was *Michaelson v. Minnesota Mining & Manufacturing Co.*, decided on July 30, 1991. They were both decided by panels of the Minnesota Court of Appeals. Each of those panels consisted of different judges. Each of those panels announced a different rule of law. Study the excerpts below (from which we have omitted various footnotes, citations, and other materials for the sake of brevity), and think about what you would do with these cases.

Hough Transit, Ltd. v. National Farmers Organization
472 N.W.2d 358 (Minn. App. 1991)
(decided on June 25, 1991, by Judges Kalitowski, Short, and Davies)

[Authors' note: Hough Transit, Ltd. ("Hough") was a trucking service hauling milk from farmers to creameries. National Farmers Organization ("the co-op") was a farmer cooperative. The cooperative had a practice of using Hough to transport its milk. In 1988, the cooperative became dissatisfied with Hough and approached one of Hough's truck drivers about the possibility of starting his own milk hauling business. The driver did so, taking over the co-op's milk routes. In subsequent litigation, Hough claimed, among other things, that the co-op had tortiously interfered with the relationship between Hough and its former driver.]

[T]he co-op cannot be liable in tort for interfering with the rights of the driver and Hough because their contract was terminable at-will. . . . Even if Minnesota were to recognize a cause of action for tortious interference with an at-will relationship, there is no evidence the co-op improperly enticed the driver away from Hough's employment. Instead, the record shows the co-op members simply asked the driver to haul the co-op routes and the driver agreed. This job offer did not rise to the level of an improper interference with Hough's relationship with the driver. . . . Under these circumstances, the trial court properly granted summary judgment [for the co-op].

Michaelson v. Minnesota Mining & Manufacturing Co.
474 N.W.2d 174 (Minn. App. 1991), *aff'd* 479 N.W.2d 58 (Minn. 1992)
(decided on July 30, 1991, by Judges Parker, Peterson, and Schultz)

[Authors' note: Minnesota Mining & Manufacturing Company ("Respondent") hired Victor Michaelson ("Appellant") to work as an attorney in the company's office of the general counsel. When the company in due course reassigned Michaelson to new job duties, he sued, alleging a variety of claims, including that coworkers tortiously interfered with his employment agreement.]

A person may be held liable for interference with a contract, however, even if the contract is terminable at will. . . . Appellant accuses his coworkers of interfering with his employment contract with respondent. These coworkers acted within their capacity as employees of respondent when they evaluated appellant's job performance and reassigned him to new duties which they believed would better serve all parties involved. We do not view such conduct as interference with appellant's employment contract. Further, even if we agreed that these workers had interfered, as agents of respondent they are protected from liability because they were acting on behalf of one party to the contract. A party cannot interfere

> with its own contract. . . . Rather, the "interferor" must be a third party. . . . The trial court properly granted summary judgment on this issue.
>
> [Authors' note: The Minnesota Supreme Court affirmed this decision, but without opinion.]

Now what do you do? The *Hough Transit* panel stated there is no such thing as a cause of action for interference with a terminable-at-will contract. The *Michaelson* panel said there is. The *Michaelson* decision did not cite *Hough*. The panels consisted of completely different judges. But the opinions are from the same court.

Step 1: Review your jurisdiction's local rules and statutes. Some jurisdictions have passed local rules or statutes to give counsel instructions concerning the handling of directly conflicting authority. If such rules or statutes exist in your jurisdiction, follow them. If no rule or statute resolves our current dilemma, what do you do?

Step 2: Look at the dates of the decisions. In general, a later case trumps an earlier one. Also, sometimes a later decision can be explained by reference to some intervening change in the law that the later decision recognizes. Neither of these considerations especially helps you decipher the present dilemma, as the two cases are only 35 days apart, and there is no legal event that explains the two different legal rule statements.

Step 3: Look to see if the later decision is a response to an invitation in the first case itself to change the law. *Hough Transit* stated that, even if Minnesota recognized a cause of action for interference, there would be nothing wrongful in the *Hough* facts. Is that statement an implied invitation to change the law? Maybe, although you might wonder why the *Michaelson* court did not even cite the *Hough* decision, if the *Michaelson* court thought *Hough* was an invitation.

Step 4: Consider whether the apparent conflict in the rules announced in the two cases is a real conflict. There is a possibility, for example, that one (or both) of two courts in an apparent direct conflict did not consider its statement of the relevant rule in question to be central to its decision. Both the *Hough Transit* panel and the *Michaelson* panel in our problem articulated alternative grounds for ruling for the defendant in their respective cases. Should either case carry more weight, then, on the question whether there is a cause of action for tortious interference with a terminable-at-will contract?

Another possibility is that the cases can be distinguished upon their material facts. Thus, the apparent conflict in rules is not a genuine one. Rather, one rule applies in one fact setting, and a different rule applies in a different fact setting. (Remember our general principle: facts drive the law.) In our case, the facts are different from those in *Hough* and *Michaelson*, but are they materially different enough to explain different rules of law on whether there is such a thing as tortious interference with a terminable-at-will contract?

Step 5: If there is a genuine, direct conflict, then is one opinion more deliberate and reasoned on the relevant point than the other is? The discussion in one decision may be more extensive, explore policy to a greater degree, compare and contrast more authority from other jurisdictions, and generally demonstrate a fuller analysis than the other. That will not particularly help you in the present circumstances, but it often can in other situations.

Step 6: If there is a genuine, direct conflict, then which opinion announces a rule that is more favorable to the resolution of your client's problem? If there is a genuine, direct conflict in authority in your jurisdiction that cannot easily be explained away, then all of your audiences are going to want to know there is such a conflict. Tell them. But then propose as the correct rule the formulation that most helps your client. You are not obligated to vote against yourself, as long as you are honest about the potential debate.

Step 7: Let policy considerations be your guide as well. The law exists to balance policy choices in resolving problems. Legal rules are always backed by policy considerations. So, in the case of two directly competing legal rule choices, which one of the formulations makes the most policy sense? Note that this may require you to review earlier decisions for explanations of relevant policies. The earlier decisions may give you insight into changing legal conditions, trends, and the like.

Template for assembling a rule in a direct conflict setting:

➤ Review the jurisdiction's local rules and statutes.
➤ Look at the dates of the decisions.
➤ Is one case a response to the other?
➤ Is there a real conflict?
➤ Is one opinion more deliberate and considered?
➤ Which case is more favorable?
➤ Consider policy implications.

How, then, should you advise your hypothetical real estate agency regarding the hiring of the employee who currently works for a competitor, assuming the only two cases on point were *Hough* and *Michaelson*? First, you would identify both cases and the apparent conflict between them. Second, you would tell the client that *Hough* is the most favorable decision in that it says there is no such thing as tortious interference with a terminable-at-will contract. Third, you would say that the apparent conflict is not a genuine one, because *Michaelson* was arguably decided on grounds not material to the present circumstances. Fourth, you would say that, even in *Michaelson*, the court thought the defendants had not committed tortious interference, and so the defense prevailed in both decisions.

ASSEMBLING RULES IN ATYPICAL SETTINGS: CASES OF FIRST IMPRESSION

Another possibility is that you are facing a legal issue on which there is no prior authority in your jurisdiction.[1] If so, you must formulate a proposed rule from persuasive authorities in other jurisdictions. The court's decision in *Horner v. Rowan Companies, Inc.,* 153 F.R.D. 597 (S.D. Tex. 1994), is a good example of the kind of analysis you will need to prepare and communicate.

Assume that you are a lawyer representing a client in a car accident case. Your client wants you to interview the doctor who examined the other

---

[1] For example, either the court must interpret a statutory provision for the first time, or the court has never addressed an issue governed by the common law.

party for injury. Your client wants you to conduct the interview *ex parte*, meaning that the other party's lawyer will not be present. You are queasy about doing this, and you research the law in your jurisdiction to see if any court decisions address the propriety of this. You find no cases. How would you advise the client?

Review the excerpted *Horner* opinion below (from which we have omitted various footnotes, citations, and other materials). The court employed the basic template for analyzing a case of first impression. You will use the same template.

Horner v. Rowan Companies, Inc.
153 F.R.D. 597 (S.D. Tex. 1994)

[Authors' note: The issue in *Horner* was whether and when defense counsel, in litigation conducted under the Federal Rules of Civil Procedure, may engage in an *ex parte* interview of a plaintiff's treating physician. The plaintiff filed his case under the Jones Act and federal maritime law for personal injury. The plaintiff had signed a broad medical release form. Relying on that form, the defendant's lawyers cancelled depositions of the plaintiff's treating physicians, and instead conducted *ex parte* interviews of them without informing plaintiff's lawyers of the latter. The plaintiff's lawyers filed a motion for sanctions against the defendant's lawyers. The federal magistrate judge assigned to the case had to decide the motion for sanctions.]

[T]he propriety of ex parte interviews of a plaintiff's treating physician by defense counsel is an unanswered question in this Circuit. The question, however, is not a new one, and of the numerous courts that have dealt with it there is no consensus. Accordingly, in its quest to establish the appropriate rule, while this Court lacks Circuit authority, it is not without the guidance and counsel of other jurists.

While the Federal Rules of Civil Procedure provide certain specific discovery devices, it is clear that no federal procedural rule explicitly permits or prohibits ex parte interviews between defendants and plaintiff's treating physicians. . . . Accordingly, federal courts that have dealt directly with this issue seem to be split. . . .

·   ·   ·

In reviewing and evaluating the various decisions, this Court has come to the conclusion that the appropriate rule should prohibit private ex parte interviews between defense counsel and plaintiff's treating physicians unless, with advance notice thereof, plaintiff specifically and unconditionally authorizes same; this is the only way in which physician patient privilege can be held inviolate.

The physician/patient privilege is recognized by Texas Rule of Evidence 509 and is adopted for use in this forum pursuant to Federal Rule of Evidence 501. . . . Quite candidly, case law and Texas Rule 509(d)(4) create an exception, or statutory waiver, of the privilege, but only as to communications or records *relevant to* the issue of a plaintiff's medical condition when litigation relative to that condition is instituted. Therefore, while there is conflicting authority, in order to preserve the integrity of the physician/patient privilege, a defendant must be limited to the formal methods of discovery enumerated by the Rules of Civil Procedure, absent the plaintiff's *express* consent to counsel's ex parte contact with his treating physicians. . . .

Unacceptable problems are inherent attendant to a contrary view. When a treating physician is interviewed ex parte by defense counsel, there are no safeguards against the revelation of matters irrelevant to the lawsuit and personally damaging to the patient, and the potential for breaches in confidentiality can have a chilling effect upon the critically important underlying relationship. Such interviews also create situations which invite questionable conduct. . . .

In answering your own question, you will adopt the same reasoning sequence.

Step 1: Determine that the relevant jurisdiction has not decided previously the legal issue. You always begin, of course, with the binding authorities in your own jurisdiction. In *Horner*, there were relevant procedural rules codifying physician-patient privilege, and cases interpreting waiver of that privilege, but none directly on point as to the interface between privilege waiver and *ex parte* interviews.

Step 2: Canvass the authorities in other jurisdictions, and apply to those authorities Steps 1 through 6 from the "direct conflict" discussion above. The authorities are merely persuasive in your setting, but they are nonetheless informative. Notice that, because the authorities elsewhere are split, you should identify and discuss the split. That is the honest way to proceed. It also gives credibility to your ultimate suggestion as to what the relevant legal rule to resolve your problem should be.

Step 3: As you canvass the authorities in other jurisdictions, pay special attention to the reasoning of those authorities. For your purposes, the reasoning is at least as important as "the rule" because, in your jurisdiction, there is no rule on point (or interpretation of a rule). Thus, a rule choice (that you are predicting a court will follow or advocating that a court ought to adopt) will need to be discussed fully.

Step 4: Analyze policy considerations. (This is Step 7 from the "direct conflict" discussion above, but it deserves independent repetition.) Especially in a case of first impression, your formulation of the relevant legal rule has to make sense from a policy standpoint. You cannot just say, "Apply the rule that our court of appeals tells us to apply." There is no such rule yet.

Step 5: Balance the policy considerations to articulate a rule. In *Horner*, for example, the court struggled to balance two competing concerns. On the one hand, the court wanted to protect doctor-patient relationships by not opening the door to defense lawyers prying into sensitive information irrelevant to a given lawsuit. On the other hand, the court wanted to preserve the right of a defendant to obtain information to defend itself. The legal compromise the court reached was to hold that a defendant can use formal discovery devices to obtain information and informal interviews if the plaintiff consents. Without the plaintiff's consent, informal interviews are forbidden.

Template for assembling rules in cases of first impression:

➢ Determine there are not cases on point in your jurisdiction.
➢ Canvass the authorities in the other jurisdictions.
➢ Apply Steps 1 through 6 from the Direct Conflict Template.
➢ Analyze the reasoning of the authorities.
➢ Analyze and balance policy considerations.
➢ In persuasive writing, focus on why the court ought to adopt a particular rule.

You will thus advise your client that the courts are split. You will tell your client that, in light of no direct precedent in your jurisdiction, reasonable lawyers may reach different conclusions concerning the propriety of *ex parte* interviews of treating physicians. You will then say that the conservative approach would be for the questioning of the doctor in your case to proceed through formal procedures.

CONCLUSION

The steps in Chapters 4, 5, and 6 will help you understand how to assemble and disassemble legal rules. The steps are useful in a wide variety of contexts. Become familiar with them, and practice them frequently. They are the building blocks of legal analysis.

CHAPTER 7

Determining the Meaning
of a Statutory Rule

At the beginning of Chapter 4, we asked you to join us in parsing the elements of Rule 3.7 of the Minnesota Rules of Professional Conduct. We then posed a problem: Suppose you are not given a rule's text. Suppose instead that you must determine what the rule is before working with it. And we identified this problem as "typical" when analyzing rules developed by court decisions rather than rules presented by enacted law, such as statutes. Chapters 4, 5, and 6 offered an approach to assembling and applying common law rules. We now turn back in this chapter to an issue unique to statutory rules—how to determine the meaning of the enacted language.

INTERPRETING STATUTORY LANGUAGE

Sometimes a statute means what it says and says what it means in unmistakable language. If so, you as a problem solver will take the language and apply it to the particular issue at hand to recommend a solution. Ultimate decision makers will do the same thing to reach a conclusion as to the recommended solution.

Sometimes, however, you are faced with statutory language that is not clear. In other words, the wording or the grammatical structure appears to create an ambiguity. One reading helps your client, a contrary reading does not. Before solving your client's problem, you will first interpret the statute before applying it to the facts of the case. The sources for interpretation that you will rely on are important because those sources determine the structure and types of arguments available to you and the other interested advocates and decision-makers.[1]

Courts look to two sources in interpreting a statute—canons of statutory construction and legislative histories. While these sources will be discussed more thoroughly in the research portion of your legal writing course, we provide a very brief overview here. A canon of statutory construction is a tool that helps a court provide meaning to the statute. There are many canons, and some contradict each other.[2] The most fundamental canon, the one that a court turns to first, is the "plain meaning rule." In applying this canon, the courts assume the legislature intended that words used in the statute be given their ordinary meaning.

When the plain meaning rule leads to illogical results or unintended consequences, then the courts will turn to other canons.[3] For example, one canon states that where general words follow specific words, then the general words should be read to include objects of a similar nature or class. To illustrate, if the statutory text refers to "cars, trucks, recreational vans, and other vehicles," the general term "other vehicles" would be read in the context of the preceding, more specific terms. Applying this canon, "other vehicles" would include any motorized vehicle, but would likely exclude non-motorized vehicles like bicycles.

---

[1] Statutory interpretation has received considerable scholarly attention. *See e.g. Symposium on Statutory Interpretation*, 53 SMU L. Rev. 3 (2000). The terms "statutory construction" and "statutory interpretation" are often used interchangeably.

[2] Karl Llewellyn, *Remarks on the Theory of Appellate Decision and the Rules or Canons About How Statutes are to be Construed*, 3 Vanderbilt L. Rev. 395 (1950).

[3] One of the more widely used resources on statutory construction is the multi-volume treatise originally authored by Jabez Gridley Sutherland and now updated by Norman J. Singer. *Sutherland Statutory Construction* (West 2002).

What sometimes happens, however, is that, even after the application of simple, threshold canons, statutory language is still ambiguous and the courts must turn to the legislative history of the statute to determine what the legislature intended when it enacted the statute. A legislative history is composed of the various documents created by the legislative body when it drafted and enacted the statute. These documents include various versions of the bill, committee and conference reports, and transcripts of hearings and debates.[4]

Understanding Issues of Statutory Interpretation in Context

To help understand how these sources are used to sort out the elements of a statute and their meaning, assume you are involved in the following case: The United States has charged your client, Mr. Gerving, with illegal possession and manufacturing of Chemical X. Chemical X has various hallucinogenic properties, and Mr. Gerving has been telling friends they can get "high" on the chemical. The United States charged Gerving with violations of 21 U.S.C. §§ 841, 844, 856, 813, and 802(32)(A). Section 813 provides:

> A controlled substance analogue shall, to the extent intended for human consumption, be treated for purposes of any Federal law as a controlled substance in schedule I.

Section 802(32)(A) defines the phrase "controlled substance analogue" as:

> The term "controlled substance analogue" means a substance—
>
> (i) the chemical structure of which is substantially similar to the chemical structure of a controlled substance in schedule I or II;

---

[4] For a more detailed discussion of the documents that comprise a legislative history, as well as the difficulties in compiling and relying on legislative histories, see Chapter 4 in Pamela Lysaght, *Michigan Legal Research* (Carolina Academic Press 2006).

(ii) which has a stimulant, depressant, or hallucinogenic effect on the central nervous system that is substantially similar to or greater than the stimulant, depressant, or hallucinogenic effect on the central nervous system of a controlled substance in schedule I or II; or

(iii) with respect to a particular person, which such person represents or intends to have a stimulant, depressant, or hallucinogenic effect on the central nervous system that is substantially similar to or greater than the stimulant, depressant, or hallucinogenic effect on the central nervous system of a controlled substance in schedule I or II.

Assume the construction of § 802(32)(A) is the sole question before the court. The government concedes that Chemical X lacks a substantially similar chemical structure to any scheduled controlled substance and that, therefore, element (i) of § 802(32)(A) is not met on the present facts. However, the government urges a disjunctive reading of the statute; i.e., the government argues that the statute requires only that (i) *or* (ii) *or* (iii) be satisfied for the substance to constitute a controlled substance analogue. From the government's perspective, because either (ii) or (iii) is present, the absence of element (i) is irrelevant to its case against Gerving.

In contrast, you, on behalf of Gerving, urge a conjunctive reading of the statute, arguing that the statute requires the government to prove (i) *and* either (ii) or (iii). Your theory is that the word "which" in each of elements (ii) and (iii) links those elements back to element (i). Under your reading of the statute, therefore, the conceded absence of element (i)—a substantially similar chemical structure to a scheduled controlled substance—is fatal to the government's case against him.

Read the following excerpt as downloaded from Westlaw. Identify which sources the court relied on and think about how to apply them in developing your argument.

U.S. v. Forbes,
806 F. Supp. 232, 234-36 (D. Colo. 1992).

     Defendants contend that this section requires a two-pronged definition. The first prong requires a substantially similar chemical structure. The second prong requires either a substantially similar effect on the human nervous system or the intent to have such an effect. The government argues that a substance may be an analogue if it satisfies any of the three clauses. I agree with defendants.

     The goal of statutory construction is to effectuate the intent and purpose of Congress. *Rocky Mountain Oil & Gas Assoc. v. Watt,* 696 F.2d 734, 745 (10th Cir.1982). Where the language of the statute itself is unambiguous, it is presumed that it expresses congressional intent and the language is controlling. *Id.* If the statutory language is unclear after resort to traditional tools of statutory construction, courts look to the legislative history to glean the intent and purpose of Congress. *235 Blum v. Stenson,* 465 U.S. 886, 896, 104 S.Ct. 1541, 1547, 79 L.Ed.2d 891 (1984); *Rocky Mountain Oil,* 696 F.2d at 745.

     The government's reading of the analogue definition has superficial appeal. As a matter of simple grammar, when an "or" is placed before the last term in a series, each term in the series is usually intended to be disjunctive. Under this reading, AET would be an analogue if it satisfies any of the three clauses. However, this reading ignores other grammatical principles that apply in favor of defendants' construction. The operative segments of clauses (ii) and (iii) both begin with the word "which", signaling the start of a dependent relative clause modifying a precedent noun. In each case, the precedent noun is "chemical structure" found in clause (i). Because both clauses (ii) and (iii) can be read to modify clause (i), the statutory language can be fairly read as requiring the two-pronged definition asserted by defendants. *See, First Charter Financial Corp. v. U.S.,* 669 F.2d 1342, 1350 (9th Cir.1982), (Modifying phrases generally refer to immediately preceding phrase). At best, the statute is ambiguous.

     Defendants' reading is also bolstered by a deeply rooted rule of statutory construction. A statute must be construed to avoid unintended or absurd results. *American Tobacco Co. v. Patterson,* 456 U.S. 63, 71, 102 S.Ct. 1534, 1538, 71 L.Ed.2d 748 (1982); *Ewing v. Rodgers,* 826 F.2d 967, 970 (10th Cir.1987). If I adopt the government's construction and read clause (ii) independently, alcohol or caffeine would be controlled substance analogues because, in concentrated form, they can have depressant or stimulant effects substantially similar to a controlled substance. Likewise, if I read clause (iii) independently, powdered sugar would be an analogue if a defendant represented that it was cocaine, effectively converting this law into a counterfeit drug statute. In both cases, a defendant could be prosecuted for selling a controlled substance analogue even though the alleged analogue did not have chemical structure substantially similar to a schedule I or II controlled substance.

Therefore, to prevent this unintended result, clause (i) must apply to any substance that the government contends is a controlled substance analogue.

Further, defendants' construction is supported by legislative history. In July, 1985, the Senate began consideration of the "Designer Drug Enforcement Act of 1985" (S.1417, later redesignated the "Controlled Substance Analog Enforcement Act of 1985", S.1437). The bill's stated purpose was "to prohibit persons who specifically set out to manufacture or to distribute drugs which are substantially similar to the most dangerous controlled substances from engaging in this activity." S.Rep. No. 196, 99th Cong., 1st Sess. 5 (1985). The Senate Judiciary Committee reported that law enforcement authorities find themselves one step behind underground chemists who slightly alter the molecular structure of controlled substances to create new drugs. *Id.* at 1-2. The Senate proposed a two-part definition of the term analogue: either the substance has a substantially similar chemical structure or it was "specifically designed" to produce an effect substantially similar to schedule I or II drugs.

In July, 1986, the House of Representatives considered the Designer Drug Enforcement Act of 1986 (H.R. 5246). As with the Senate, the House bill focused on underground chemists who seek to evade the drug laws by slightly altering a controlled substance. H.R.Rep. No. 948, 99th Cong., 2d Sess. 4 (1986). The House proposed a two-pronged definition of analogue that is virtually identical to the construction advocated by defendants here. The House bill contained the same three clauses as the current statute, but added the word "and" after clause (i).

> The term "controlled substance analogue" is defined to conform
> as closely as possible to the policy of the Controlled Substances
> Act by *requiring a chemical relationship to a substance which
> is controlled* ⋯ *and either* the existence of some stimulant,
> depressant, or hallucinogenic effect on the central nervous system,
> or a representation or intent that the substance have a stimulant,
> depressant, or hallucinogenic effect substantially *236* similar to,
> or greater than, such effect of any controlled substance.

Id. at 2, (emphasis added). The report illustrates the point with coffee. "Coffee, for example, has a stimulant effect on the central nervous system, but it is not chemically substantially similar to a controlled substance." *Id.* at 7.

Congress ultimately adopted the analogue statute as part of the comprehensive "Anti-Drug Abuse Act of 1986" (H.R. 5484). Inexplicably, the analogue definition enacted by Congress dropped the word "and" after clause (i). Otherwise, that definition and the two-pronged definition considered by the House are virtually identical. I consider the House report to be persuasive legislative history as to Congress' intent underlying its definition of a controlled substance analogue.

> The legislative history thus clearly supports defendants' construction. The analogue statute is directed at underground chemists who tinker with the molecular structure of controlled substances to create new drugs that are not scheduled. If a substance could be an analogue without a substantially similar chemical structure, Congress' stated purpose would be significantly expanded. Moreover, by essentially adopting the House definition, Congress evidenced its intent to require a two-pronged definition.
>
> $\cdot \quad \cdot \quad \cdot$
>
> Finally, courts must construe criminal statutes narrowly in favor of lenity to the accused. *United States v. Enmons,* 410 U.S. 396, 411, 93 S.Ct. 1007, 1015, 35 L.Ed.2d 379 (1973); *Mahn v. Gunter,* 978 F.2d 599 (10th Cir.1992), (Rule of lenity is a doctrine of last resort in statutory construction). Although it is not necessary to apply this rule as a last resort, its application yields a result entirely consistent with defendants' construction. The two-pronged definition not only promotes lenity in this prosecution, but narrows future analogue prosecutions to only those cases where the substance has a chemical structure substantially similar to a schedule I or II controlled substance. Therefore, I hold that a substance may be a controlled substance analogue only if it satisfies clause (i) *and* clauses (ii) *or* (iii).

The court in *Forbes* was engaged in a classic statutory construction. When you develop statutory arguments, you will follow the same sequence the court used.

Step 1: Determine if the questionable words can be given their ordinary meaning. In *Forbes,* the court looked to the ordinary meaning as well as the grammatical structure of the statute. It ruled that these tools rendered the statute ambiguous.

Step 2: Search for other canons that support your client's interpretation. Pay particular attention to which canons the courts in your jurisdiction apply to ambiguous statutes. If those canons help your adversary, be honest in recognizing them. Chances are, however, that you will be able to distinguish the canon or find others that support your position. If in doubt about that, just scan the "thrusts" and "parries" identified in the Llewellyn article.[5]

---

[5] *See supra* n. 2.

Step 3: Canvass the documents that comprise the legislative history. Determine which ones support your interpretation and which do not. Emphasize those sources that favor your interpretation, and distinguish those that do not. Some sources are more persuasive—various drafts of the bill and committee and conference reports.

Step 4: Look for the underlying policy considerations that helped to drive the legislation in the first place. What problem was the legislature intending to address? In *Forbes*, the court noted Congress' desire to reach underground chemists who molecularly alter controlled substances to create new designer drugs. Focusing on these policy considerations is a way to distinguish between legislative history sources that offer competing interpretations.

Step 5: When interpreting criminal statutes, note that there is an additional canon that can be raised as a final argument—the Rule of Lenity. The *Forbes* court invoked this rule to support its holding. But note if you are the government, not all is lost. The rule is not consistently applied. Thus, as the government, you would discuss those cases in which the rule was not applied or rejected.

Does your client, Gerving, have a strong argument, based on the canons, legislative history, and policy considerations? Certainly under *Forbes*. Of course, it is always helpful when other courts have interpreted the statute—and even more helpful when they have done so in a way that supports your interpretation. When there are no cases, however, you will need to go through these steps, searching the canons and the legislative history to develop your position.

What to Avoid in Statutory Interpretation

First, even if you have a strong plain meaning argument, do not stop there. The opposing party likely will argue that the plain meaning leads to illogical or unintended results and, therefore, additional canons must be consulted as well as the legislative history. Therefore, look for canons and legislative history that support your plain meaning, even though technically the court should not look to additional canons and the legislative history if the plain meaning resolves the issue. By developing these "even if" arguments, you are countering your opponent's position.

Second, and somewhat inconsistently, appreciate that not *all* judges favor delving into legislative histories. Some judges will resist turning to legislative histories because they view the process as dubious, i.e. it is too easy for lawyers to select only bits of legislative history that favor their own clients instead of representative legislative history as a whole. The judges prefer to focus on the words used in the statute.[6]

CONCLUSION

When faced with statutory language that is not clear, the problem solver must look to canons of statutory construction and the legislative history. Additionally, developing the solution requires employing a specific method of analysis.

---

[6] Remember that as an officer of the court, you have an obligation to be honest about legislative history—even as a zealous advocate.

CHAPTER 8

Basic Organizing Principles in Legal Analysis and Writing

There are several ways to structure your thinking about legal problems so as to facilitate solving the problems and presenting the analyses to readers. One approach is well known under the acronym IRAC, which stands for Introduction,[1] Rule, Application, and Conclusion.[2] Properly understood and

---

[1] We have adopted the formula where the "I" stands for "Introduction" rather than "Issue," which was suggested by Professor Christina Kunz and Associate Dean Deborah Schmedemann in *Point/Counterpoint: Use of IRAC-type Formulas—Desirable or Dangerous?* 10 The Second Draft 11 (Nov. 1995) (bulletin of the Leg. Writing Inst.) [hereinafter *Point/Counterpoint*], and more fully developed in their text, *Synthesis: Legal Reading, Reasoning, and Writing* 119-20 (Aspen L. & Bus. 1999). The Introduction does, of course, introduce a reader to an issue; but it also may involve a broader explanation of a relevant problem to be solved and a proposed potential solution.

[2] Because so many legal writing professionals have written about the IRAC formula and similar analytical paradigms, much of our discussion in this chapter is necessarily derivative. We gratefully acknowledge those colleagues whose discussions of IRAC and IRAC-type formulae helped shape and refine our own views: Charles R. Calleros, *Legal Method and Writing* 69-95, 199, 222, 332 (4th ed., Aspen L. & Bus. 2002); Linda Holdeman Edwards, *Legal Writing:*

executed, the IRAC formula is a helpful device in thinking about and solving legal problems because it replicates the way in which lawyers approach solving problems: gather the facts to identify the issue, identify the governing rules, analyze the problem in light of the rules and the client's facts, conclude the analysis.[3]   It helps in communicating the solution—the analysis—because it provides a basic framework that is audience focused and reader friendly.[4]

Moreover, the IRAC formula is consistent with the syllogism paradigm so common to legal argument.[5]   As you may recall from your undergraduate education, a syllogism consists of a major premise, a minor premise, and a conclusion that flows as a logical consequence from the premises. One of the most classic examples of a syllogism is the following:

> Major Premise: All men are mortal.
> Minor Premise: Socrates was a man.
> Conclusion: Therefore, Socrates was mortal.

In the legal context, the major premise is the rule; the minor premise consists of the facts; and the resolution, the "therefore," is the conclusion. This is, of course, oversimplified. But our point is that syllogisms can be expressed through an IRAC structure.

Process, Analysis, Organization 85-127 (3d ed., Aspen L. & Bus. 2002); Richard K. Neumann, Jr., *Legal Reasoning & Legal Writing: Structure, Strategy, & Style* 95-118 (4th ed., Aspen L. & Bus. 2001); Diana V. Pratt, *Legal Writing: A Systematic Approach* 88-106, 167-75 (3d ed., West 1999); Nancy L. Schultz & Louis J. Sirico, Jr., *Legal Writing & Other Lawyering Skills* 37-65 (3d ed., Matthew Bender 1998); and Kunz & Schmedemann, *supra* n. 1.

[3] *See* Amy E. Sloan, *Erasing Lines: Integrating the Law School Curriculum*, 1 J. ALWD 3, 3-4 & n. 4 (2002) (discussing how syllogisms and the IRAC formula are taught in first-year doctrinal and writing courses as a problem-solving methodology).

[4] The IRAC formula is not the exclusive device for thinking about and presenting a legal analysis, nor is it without controversy. Critics complain that it is too formulaic, overly simplistic, rigid, and misleading; advocates claim it is flexible, adaptable, and a powerful organizing tool. *See Point/Counterpoint, supra* n. 1, at 1-20.

[5] For an in-depth and informative discussion of how syllogistic—or enthymematic—reasoning is similar to legal reasoning, see Steven D. Jamar, *Aristotle Teaches Persuasion: The Psychic Connection*, 8 Scribes J. Leg. Writing 61 (2001-2002).

Further, the IRAC formula is suitable for predictive writing—for example, predicting to another lawyer or a client how a court is likely to rule on a particular issue—as well as for persuasive writing—for example, persuading a court to rule favorably for your client. Although both types of writing involve arguments, predictive writing is presented objectively and persuasive writing is presented through advocacy.

Finally, the IRAC formula works at macro and micro organizational levels. The IRAC formula is best explained at the macro level in the context of the more common types of documents lawyers prepare: office memoranda, client letters, and trial and appellate briefs. (There are many other types of documents that lawyers prepare, including transactional documents like contracts, but our focus is on the most typical documents explored within a first-year legal writing course as vehicles to communicate the resolution to a problem.) In each of these documents, the lawyer must introduce the problem to be resolved, explain the relevant rule that governs the problem, apply the rule to the client's facts, and provide the conclusion. In this respect, the analysis section of a memorandum, the body of a client letter, and the argument sections of a trial brief and an appellate brief contain a macro IRAC.

Often, however, there are multiple problems—or issues—that must be addressed. The IRAC formula also works at the micro level. Each discrete issue, sub-issue, or element can usually be presented in an IRAC formula. Developing one issue, sub-issue, or element in a separate IRAC formula can be helpful to the novice legal writer who does not know where to begin. But it is only a beginning. The full analysis must be woven together so as to create a tapestry—a picture for the audience. Discrete IRACs must be carefully meshed together, which is usually achieved through transitions and bridges between the discrete IRACs. More will be said later about how to create these transitions and bridges.

All of these reasons account for the IRAC formula's continued vitality. The key to its proper use is to know the basic IRAC components and how to adapt them for different types of legal reasoning. In this way, you will be able to capitalize on the IRAC formula's strengths while minimizing its limitations. The remainder of this chapter discusses how to work with the IRAC formula in both predictive and persuasive writing.

The basic components described below are intended to apply to the analysis section of a memorandum, body of a client letter, and argument sections of trial and appellate briefs. In Chapters 11 and 12, you will see how the IRAC formula works in context.[6] Unfortunately, although we discuss below the IRAC components and how to adapt them, the discussion is unavoidably abstract, even with simple examples. You must practice working with the IRAC formula in the context of solving legal problems. Mastering the IRAC formula, like much of legal analysis and writing, is an acquired skill. If you would like to see a picture of what the IRAC formula might look like in practice before you read the discussion below, look at the outline on page 95 of this chapter.

IRAC: THE BASIC COMPONENTS

1. Introduction

The first step in analyzing and presenting a legal analysis is to identify the issue—the problem that must be solved. Because the legal reading audience does *not want to wait* in suspense to see how the analytical story ends—or how the problem is resolved—legal writers also provide a statement of the conclusion in the introduction, unless there is a unique reason not to do so. The audience wants to know what to do. Identifying the problem without identifying a solution is less than fully satisfactory.

There is also a practical reason for including a statement of the conclusion: You want your reader to *understand* where you are going—even when your analysis aims simply at an objective prediction of how a court would likely rule if faced with your client's issue. By stating your conclusion in your introduction of the issue, the reader can more easily follow your reasoning, which you then present in your discussion of the relevant rule and its application to the client's facts.

The same is true in persuasive (as opposed to objective) writing. In writing briefs to the trial court or appellate court, legal writers begin with an

---

[6] You may also want to refer back to Chapter 1, which covers road mapping. Note the use of an IRAC formula in constructing the micro road map of the analysis in *Bear v. Gold*.

assertion of one of their arguments. (Typically, there is more than one issue before the court, and each issue may have—will likely have—more than one argument.) This assertion is made through a point heading, which we describe in Chapter 12. A major point heading typically functions as an overall introduction to the arguments for a particular issue. The minor point headings typically serve to introduce the discrete arguments for that issue.

Introductions in both predictive and persuasive legal writing may also serve to provide general background information for context. Similarly, the introduction may include a basic road map of the analysis or argument that follows. In developing your introductions, consider the following questions.

> **Is the document making a prediction, such as in an office memorandum or client letter?**

➤ Is the problem you are analyzing clearly stated, either as an issue or as a thesis statement?

➤ Is the conclusion stated, either separately from the issue or in the thesis statement?

➤ If a fairly lengthy analysis will follow, is a brief background discussion required to provide a context for understanding the analysis that follows?

➤ Are there several rules or elements that will be provided, explained, and applied in the rule and application sections, requiring a general road map of the analysis?

➤ Is there any other reason to expand the introduction so as to assist the reader in following your predictive analysis?

> **Is the document intended to persuade, such as a trial or appellate brief?**

➤ Are there assertions, theses, or conclusions stated in the major point headings that begin the specific arguments addressing the identified issues?

➤ Are there additional, discrete arguments requiring their own minor point headings?

➤ Would background information after the major point heading and before the minor point headings provide needed context or an overview?

➤ Is there any other reason to expand the introduction so as to assist the reader in following your argument?

The following examples demonstrating the basic composition of each section of the IRAC formula are based on an office memorandum analyzing a potential forcible confinement kidnapping case against a suspect. Although there are four elements in the statute, we present in this discussion only one of the elements and the facts easily satisfy the statutory requirement.

In the following example, the introduction captures the issue (was Mr. Mokely forcibly confined) and the conclusion (yes) in one sentence as a thesis statement:

Ms. Nars forcibly confined Mr. Mokely within the meaning of the statute.

---

2. Rule

The legal writer must next provide the governing rule. This sounds simple enough in theory, but it can be fairly complex in practice because there are a number of considerations. In predictive and persuasive legal writing, the legal writer has to demonstrate why the rule governs the problem and has to provide an explanation of how the rule works. The former can sometimes be done through citation to the rule, especially when the rule is mandatory in the jurisdiction. At other times, a discussion of the source of the rule, and its persuasive value, may be necessary. The explanation of the rule can be fairly straight forward, demonstrating how a court has applied the rule in a factually similar problem. Or, the explanation can be quite elaborate, involving synthesizing various cases.

In general, when there is a statutory or common law rule to apply, but it is not "at issue," then the rule section part of the IRAC template may be very short, requiring nothing more than a quotation or a paraphrase and a citation demonstrating that the relevant specific legal rule governs this problem. By "not at issue," we mean that, even though you have to demonstrate that your client fulfilled this statutory or common law obligation so she can, for example, proceed in seeking a remedy, the legal rule itself will be taken as a given and will not be the focus of the legal challenge. It is merely a stepping-stone in the analysis.

Conversely, there are a number of settings where the relevant legal rule is the focus of challenge. One common example arises when a legal rule is ambiguous, and there is a question as to how to interpret it. In such a scenario, the rule section within the IRAC template will often be fairly elaborate. In addition to providing the rule and a citation, it may be necessary to explain the rule by discussing cases in which the courts have interpreted the rule in other factual contexts. Another common example arises when a court must adopt a particular rule among competing rules. In this setting, which most typically arises in the context of issues of first impression, it is helpful to have an expansive "rule" section within the IRAC structure that focuses on the reasons for adopting a specific rule. As such, the reasoning from those courts that have adopted the rule is helpful in fleshing out this section.

Not surprisingly, a common problem we see in students' papers is incomplete rule sections. An incomplete rule section will almost always result in a faulty and an incomplete application section. The rule section is the foundation for the application. To avoid the problem of incomplete rule sections, determine how much more information must be supplied for the reader to understand the rule. As you work through your legal writing problems, you will become proficient at determining the depth of treatment required in various contexts. Here is a list of questions to help you get started.

> **Does the rule come from enacted law?**

➢ Is there more than one rule that must be discussed?

➢ Are there multiple elements? Does each element need to be discussed separately?

➢ Do any of the terms need to be explained by demonstrating how other courts have applied them to similar factual contexts?

➢ Are any of the terms ambiguous? How have the courts interpreted those ambiguous terms?

➢ Are there policy considerations—either by the legislative body that enacted the rule or the judicial body that interpreted and applied it—that need to be explained?

Does the rule come from the common law?

> Are any cases controlling, i.e., mandatory authority? How do you need to demonstrate that?
> If not, is the authority analogous? How will you demonstrate that?
> Is it necessary to discuss the cases in some detail so the reader understands how the courts applied the rule?
> How is the court's reasoning important to understanding the rule?
> If the rule has evolved from a series of cases, how will you synthesize the cases to formulate a statement of the rule?
> What are the policy implications that need to be discussed?

Is this an issue of first impression for the court?

> How has the court decided similar issues?
> How have courts in other jurisdictions decided the issue?
> Is there a "majority" and "minority" rule or interpretation?
> What was the reasoning of the courts in adopting one rule or interpretation over another?
> How does this reasoning help in determining which rule or interpretation your jurisdiction will adopt (in predictive writing) or ought to adopt (in persuasive writing)?

Example of a rule requiring only a brief explanation:

For a charge of forcible confinement kidnapping, the State must prove beyond a reasonable doubt that the defendant "forcibly . . . confine[d] or imprison[ed]" the victim. Mich. Comp. Laws Ann. § 750.349 (West 1992). This element has been defined as "an unlawful seizure of a person against his will." *People v. Wesley*, 365 N.W.2d 692, 695 (Mich. 1984). Using a weapon forcibly to detain a person satisfies this element. For example, in *People v. Worden*, 248 N.W.2d 597 (Mich. App. 1977), the defendant held a gun on his victim, robbed him, and ordered him into the defendant's car. The victim was released approximately one-quarter of a mile down the road.

---

3. *Application*

The legal writer must apply the rule to the facts of the problem. Again, this sounds simple enough in the abstract, but, like the rule section, it can be highly nuanced. Some novice legal writers merely state that if the court applies the rule, then the client will prevail. That is not what we mean by "apply." The application of the rule to the facts is the written expression of the legal reasoning process—be it predictive or persuasive.

In general, when the rule is from enacted law or the common law and is not at issue, the legal writer may properly provide only a short statement of the facts to demonstrate that the requirements of the rule are met. This would be an example of straightforward deductive reasoning.

Suppose the legal rule is not at issue, but there is a question as to whether the facts are sufficient to meet the legal standard, either from statutory or common law. In this situation, the legal writer likely will need to compare and contrast the facts and reasoning from the cases initially identified in the rule section to the instant facts.

Sometimes, however, counsel for each side is instead advocating the application of a different rule or a different interpretation of a rule. In these situations, the rule section identifies reasons the court should adopt one rule or interpretation over another. The application section will link those reasons to policy considerations and the instant facts.

It may be necessary before concluding to present any counter-analysis. In predictive writing, an objective analysis requires consideration of the opposing arguments. Depending upon the context, the counter-analysis may be addressed within a single "application" section. In other situations, it may be necessary to develop a separate IRAC to address the counter-analysis. Suppose, for example, that there is an issue concerning which of two competing rules governs the dispute. (Some of the ways that this can occur include situations where the facts are in dispute and therefore it is not clear which rule applies, in splits of authority within a jurisdiction, and in issues of first impression within a jurisdiction.) One line of authority could be developed under one IRAC; and the other line of authority—the one you are rejecting—could be developed in a separate IRAC.

Counter-arguments are very common to brief writing. A question often arises as to where to include the counter-argument. If the point made in the counter-argument is directly related to the discrete argument being advanced, then the counter-argument can be placed within the rule section, the application section, or potentially both. If, however, the counter-argument needs considerable development, then it may be best to provide a separate IRAC.

A common problem among novice legal writers is a disembodied application section: The writer discusses the facts of her problem and never makes reference to the rules, cases, reasoning, or policies discussed in the rule section. It is the writer's job to connect the threads between the rules and the facts—to weave the analysis. Here are some considerations to keep in mind when crafting application sections.

> **Is there a question as to whether the instant facts satisfy the rule?**

➤ Is it necessary to compare and contrast the facts and reasoning of other cases with the instant facts?

➤ When comparing the cases, are there logical links for the legal reader so that she can easily understand how the factual similarities between and among the cases justify a similar result in the instant case?

➤ Conversely, if it is necessary to contrast cases, are the factual differences between and among the cases fully developed so as to justify why there should be a dissimilar result in the instant case?

> **Is there a question as to which rule or interpretation of a rule the court should apply?**

➤ Is the reasoning discussed in the rule section logically linked and applied to the instant situation?

➤ Are there policy considerations that should be expanded upon?

> **Is a counter-analysis (predictive writing) or counter-argument (persuasive writing) necessary?**

➤ Is the competing rule or interpretation adequately and accurately developed?

➢ Is a discussion of cases necessary so as to properly counter the competing rule or interpretation?

➢ Are there logical links to the instant facts demonstrating why this rule or interpretation is wrong or undesirable?

Example of a fairly short application requiring minimal comparison to another case:

Similar to the defendant in *Worden,* who was convicted, Ms. Nars held a gun to Mr. Mokely's head and ordered him to drive down the road. Mr. Mokely's forcible confinement is further evidenced by his taped testimony: He repeatedly offered Ms. Nars his car and pleaded with her to let him go. But Ms. Nars continued to hold the gun to Mr. Mokely's head and threatened him by yelling, "Shut up or I'll kill you!"

---

4. Conclusion

Just as in the syllogism, the conclusion should follow from the application of the rule to the facts. The conclusion may be very brief, as in the case of a single issue and single governing statutory provision or common law rule, or the conclusion may have to bring together competing rules and applications. There are, of course, other possibilities. Our point is that writing the conclusion, just like writing the introduction, rule, and application sections, requires looking at the context of the problem and analysis. For example, conclusions to discrete analyses and arguments are not always necessary. In fact, if every discrete analysis or argument in a series of analyses or arguments contains a conclusion, the effect may appear stilted. On the other hand, a lengthy analysis or argument may need summation.

Example of a very short conclusion:

The State will be able to meet its burden on this element because . . .

LINKING DISCRETE IRACs

There may be multiple IRACs within the analysis section of the memorandum, the body of the client letter, and the argument sections of trial and appellate briefs. When an entire issue or argument can be discussed in one IRAC, then there is often no need to link to other IRACs, even where there are other issues and arguments. This is because each issue in a memorandum and each argument in a brief should be identified through headings (memoranda) or point headings (briefs), which also serve as transitions. Often, however, a single issue may need several IRACs to flesh out the complete analysis because there may be discrete rules or separate elements that have to be applied.

The following outline demonstrates how the examples used above might fit within the broader context of the analysis section of an office memorandum addressing all the elements of the statute. The outline also illustrates a macro IRAC formula composed of discrete micro IRACs.

ANALYSIS SECTION	CONTENT
I: *Overall Introduction*	• Thesis statement. (The facts support a charge of forcible confinement kidnapping against Ms. Nars.) • Full text of material provisions of statute. • Specific elements for forcible confinement kidnapping.
R: *Overall Rule and* **A: *Application Sections***	(Each element could be set off with a separate mini heading.) **I:** Thesis statement regarding first element (forcible confinement). **R:** Statutory requirement (it would not be necessary to repeat the statutory language); court's definition; an example. **A:** Apply language and definition to instant facts; analogize to similar case. **C:** Briefly conclude analysis for this element.
	I: Thesis statement regarding second element (willfully, maliciously, and without legal authority). **R:** Statutory requirement; discuss cases applying element. **A:** Apply to instant facts; analogize and distinguish as necessary. **C:** Briefly conclude analysis for this element.
	I: Thesis statement regarding third element (against the will of the person confined). **R:** Statutory requirement; discuss cases applying element. Identify rule relating to potential defense of consent; discuss cases applying defense. **A:** Apply third element to instant facts; analogize and distinguish as necessary. **Counter-analysis:** Apply potential defense to instant facts. **C:** Briefly conclude analysis for this element.
	I: Thesis statement regarding fourth element (an asportation not merely incidental to the underlying crime). **R:** Statutory requirement; asportation defined and relevant factors provided; discuss cases applying element. **A:** Apply to instant facts; analogize and distinguish as necessary. **C:** Briefly conclude analysis for this element.
Conclusion	Implied from the conclusions in the discrete IRACs. (The formal Conclusion would provide a brief summation of the analysis for each element.)

In some situations, it is necessary to link the discrete IRACs with topic sentences, because the analysis does not lend itself to providing mini headings. The introduction section often serves as the bridge or link, because it can provide the next topic, a thesis, or the conclusion. In the latter situation, another conclusion at the end is often not necessary.[7]

The following example from an office memorandum is based on a problem involving the sale of goods and includes the following facts.

> Buyer manufactures military apparel. Buyer entered into a contract with Seller of cotton cording, which is used in manufacturing the military apparel. Seller failed to deliver the cotton cording, causing Buyer to breach its contract with another company for which it was manufacturing the military apparel. Buyer incurred consequential damages. Is Seller liable for Buyer's losses?

This issue requires application of more than one statutory provision from Article 2 of the *Uniform Commercial Code*. We will not take you through the entire analysis here, but five of the statutory requirements that would be discussed in the sequence would demonstrate that Article 2 governs this transaction, or, more properly, a state's enactment of Article 2 governs this transaction, because the cotton cording is a "good," there was a written contract between the parties, and the action is not time barred. There is no "issue" as to whether this is a transaction in goods, that the cotton cording meets the definition of goods, that there was a written contract, or that the action is not time barred. But each of these statutory requirements should be discussed to demonstrate that they are not at issue. This can be accomplished through simple deductive analysis using the IRAC formula.

---

[7] *See* Kunz & Schmedemann, *Point/Counterpoint*, *supra*, n. 1, at 11 (explaining that the Introduction in an IRAC may consist of "an issue, transition, topic, thesis, or conclusion").

> **Example of linking IRACs:**
>
> Section 2-102 states that Article 2 "applies to transactions in goods . . . ." The term "goods" is defined in section 2-105 as "all things (including specially manufactured goods) which are movable at the time of identification to the contract for sale . . . ." The cotton cording is a good within the meaning of the statute; thus Article 2 governs this transaction.
>
> Buyer and Seller contracted on January 25, 200x, for the sale of the cotton cording. Section 2-204(1) states that "[a] contract for sale may be made in any manner to show agreement." The Parties' contract consists of a purchase order from Buyer and a signed acceptance letter agreeing to all the terms of Buyer's purchase order, which satisfies section 2-204. This writing also satisfies the statute of frauds under section 2-201, which requires that sales of goods for $500 and more have "some writing sufficient to indicate that a contract for sale has been made between the parties and signed by the party against whom enforcement is sought . . . ."
>
> Buyer currently has more than three years to bring suit against Seller. Section 2-725(1) provides that unless the parties contracted otherwise, "[a]n action for breach of any contract for sale must be commenced within four years after the cause of action has accrued." Subsection (2) states that the "cause of action accrues when the breach occurs, regardless of the aggrieved party's lack of knowledge of the breach." The contract between Buyer and Seller did not alter the four-year statute of limitations. The contract date for delivery was March 17, 200x.
>
> Buyer's general remedies are set forth in Section 2-711. . . .

When linking discrete IRACs, be careful not to adhere too technically to the IRAC formula because you could lose sight of the bigger picture—communicating with your audience. IRAC after IRAC after IRAC can become tedious to the reader. Modify the introduction and conclusion sections as needed to provide a flow to your prose, without sacrificing the analysis.

Furthermore, when communicating your analysis, do not describe your analytical process. Instead, provide your analysis—the resolution to the legal problem. Many novice legal writers make the mistake of describing what they are doing, erroneously thinking that a description of their process serves as a transition.[8] Statements such as "now I will discuss the relevant rules" or "now it is important to analogize the instant facts to the facts of three cases" are examples of describing the analytical process. Instead, provide transitions that substantively move the analysis forward: "This transaction is governed by California's enactment of Article 2 of the *Uniform Commercial Code*." "The facts in [case name and citation] are similar to the instant facts. In [case] . . . ."[9]

CONCLUSION

Learn to work with the IRAC formula—or, more aptly, learn to make it work for you. The IRAC formula can be useful in organizing a complex analysis. But beware: If you apply it rotely, then your analysis and communication will suffer.

---

[8] Pamela Lysaght is grateful to her colleague, Professor Cristina Lockwood, for her insightful description of this common mistake first-year students make while grappling with setting forth their analyses.

[9] Rarely is it appropriate to use "Rule" and "Application" as mini-headings in the analysis section of a memorandum, the body of a client letter, or the argument sections of trial and appellate briefs.

CHAPTER 9

Basic Writing Principles

There are many books on the market that discuss writing style. We have referred over time to such texts (in alphabetical order) as:

- Anne Enquist & Laurel Currie Oates, *Just Writing* (Aspen L. & Bus. 2001).
- Bryan A. Garner, *The Redbook: A Manual on Legal Style* (West 2002).
- Bryan A. Garner, *The Winning Brief* (Oxford U. Press 1999).
- C. Edward Good, *Mightier than the Sword* (1989).
- Terri LeClercq, *Guide to Legal Writing Style* (2d ed., Aspen L. & Bus. 2000).
- William Strunk Jr. & E.B. White, *The Elements of Style* (4th ed., Longman 2000).
- Joseph M. Williams, *Style* (6th ed., Longman 2000).
- Richard C. Wydick, *Plain English for Lawyers* (4th ed., Carolina Academic Press 1998).

Any readers who wish detailed advice on stylistic matters can profit from reviewing one or more of these books. In various ways, they contain the advice in this chapter. We make no claim of great original insight into the thoughts below. We assume, however, that our audience (busy first-year law students) may not always take the time to review separately the above or other texts. And there are certain basic principles that beginning legal writers must absorb until the principles are second nature. So we set those out below for convenient reference.

> **Prefer Simplicity**

Principle No. 1: Keep your writing simple. Great communicators take complex topics and reduce them to simple components that are easily understood.

This is not the same thing as "dumbing down" your writing. Dumbing down your language implies pejoratively that the audience is too stupid to understand a sophisticated approach to communication. As a legal writer, you cannot afford such a condescending attitude. For one thing, a lot of legal audiences are well educated and smart. For another, when you are writing to clients, judges, colleagues, and opposing lawyers, you are seeking to convey a proposed solution to a problem—*a solution that they are not obligated to accept.* Clients can fire you. Judges can rule against you. Colleagues can refuse to work with you. Opposing lawyers can go out of their way to make your life miserable. None of these persons wants you to talk down to them. So by saying "keep it simple," we are not directing you to be condescending. Instead, we are saying that your audience members are likely to be busy people, with too much to do in too little time. If you give them unnecessary complexity, they will ignore you, or worse. They want answers to problems, and they want the answers in a form that it will be easy for all of the necessary actors to understand and adopt.

Be aware also that making complex topics simple is a difficult business. A writer cannot do that unless and until he thoroughly understands the relevant problem, the applicable legal principles, the material facts, and his proposed solution. In our experience, it is often *harder* to be simple than to be complex. Thus, the "keep it simple" rule is not a formula for lax work habits either.

Prefer the Familiar

Principle No. 2: Help the reader through the use of familiar words, concepts, and analogies. This is a corollary to the first rule. Audiences like to see terms, ideas, and comparisons about which they already know something. So, if you have a choice between a big word that the audience will have to look up and a familiar word that the audience already knows, then pick the latter, all other things being equal. Similarly, if you can explain a complicated new idea by drawing an analogy to something the reader already understands, do so; it will help the communication process.

Prefer Concision

Principle No. 3: Express your thoughts in the fewest words that are adequate to cover the subject matter. Prefer short words. Prefer short sentences (no more than twenty to twenty-five words). Prefer short paragraphs (no more than eight to ten sentences). Prefer short documents. Your audience members are busy. Get to the solution to the relevant legal problem as quickly as possible, and then get out!

Recall, however, that your audience members want your writing to be interesting. Not *every* word in the document you are writing should be short. Not *every* sentence should be twenty words. Not *every* paragraph should be eight sentences. Variety is important.

Prefer Action

Principle No. 4: Emphasize action to keep your audience's attention. This means emphasize verbs, particularly active verbs (e.g., "the court decided that . . . ." in preference to "the court's decision was that . . . .") Prefer active voice (e.g., "Robert sued William" in preference to "William was sued by Robert"). Short, simple, active sentences will keep your audience focused upon the unfolding scene (e.g., "Jane hit the ball. The ball smashed through Robert's window. Robert stormed out of the house.")

Note, however, that there are times when you want variation. For example, the use of passive voice ("William was sued by Robert") may be ideal when you want the attention of the reader focused upon the recipient of the action, rather than upon the actor. Indeed, you may have reasons for not wanting to name the actor at all ("William was sued"). So we are not saying *only* use active verbs and active voice. We are stating a preference, albeit an important one, not an absolutely infallible rule.

Avoid Overuse of Adjectives and Adverbs

Principle No. 5: Let nouns and verbs do most of your talking, not adjectives and adverbs. Particularly avoid exaggeration through conclusory modifiers such as "clearly," "plainly," "very," "obviously," "outrageous," "unconscionable," and the like. Recall that lawyers must get used to living with ambiguity much of the time. Reasonable people can often disagree about what the real problem is that needs to be resolved, what the law says or should say about the problem, what the facts are, and what the solution should be. As a result, it is often hard to say credibly that an answer is "plain," or that particular conduct is "outrageous," or that facts are "very clear." So avoid saying those things.

Pay Attention to Flow

Principle No. 6: Pay attention to the flow of your sentences. Modifying clauses are least disruptive to the flow of your thoughts if they come at the beginning or the end of a sentence, rather than in the middle. Consider the following example:

> ➤ Even if it is a remote one, the possibility must be considered.
> ➤ The possibility, even if it is a remote one, must be considered.
> ➤ The possibility must be considered, even if it is a remote one.

The middle example is generally less effective than the other two. Why? Because the middle example appears choppy. Lead or conclude with the language that you want your reader to think about the most—in this example, that the possibility must be considered.

Note, however, that there may be times when you want the reader to pause on the interrupting clause. (In fact, you will see examples in this text.)

Be Meticulous

Principle No. 7: Pay attention to detail. The credibility of a legal writing piece and of the writer suffer dramatically when the writer is sloppy.

> ➤ Be precise in your wording of, and citations to, facts and rules.
> ➤ Use correct grammar.
> ➤ Use correct punctuation.
> ➤ Proofread your writing carefully.
> ➤ If there are court rules, office rules, client rules, or the like that apply to the document, make sure you follow them.
> ➤ If there is a deadline for handing in the work product, meet it.

In other words, be careful in small things because, if you are not careful in small things, then your audience will not trust you on the large ones.

COMMON MISTAKES TO AVOID

The following are the most common editing corrections that we have to make. Try to avoid these mistakes:

> ➤ "**It's**" is the abbreviation for "it is." "**It's**" is NOT the possessive form of the word "it." If you want the possessive of the word "it," then you use the word "**Its**." Example: <The car's motor is not

running properly.> <Its motor is not running properly.> <It's not running properly.>

➤ A corporation or other entity is an "**it**," NOT a "they." Example: <Acme announced its year-end stock dividend.> <It announced its year-end stock dividend.>

➤ Do not mix verb tenses. If you are using the past tense to describe action in a paragraph, do NOT suddenly switch over to present tense to describe the same action. Example: <The court announced a rule of lenity. The court resolved the doubt over the meaning of the law in favor of the defendant.> NOT: <The court announced a rule of lenity. The court resolves the doubt over the meaning of the law in favor of the defendant.> More important, discuss cases in the past tense because the case has been decided. But discuss current statutes in the present tense.

➤ Watch out for ambiguous pronouns. A pronoun ordinarily refers to the preceding noun. In sentences that use multiple nouns, the pronouns can be confusing. Example: <Mary was with Sally when she bought a gift at the department store. She mailed it to Robert.> Does the first "she" refer to Sally or Mary? How about the second "she"? Does the "it" refer to the department store or the gift? (In context, the reader may be able to determine that one meaning of an ambiguous pronoun is nonsensical. For example, Sally is not likely to be mailing a department store to Robert. But deciphering the correct reference is not always that easy, and, in any event, why make the reader go through the work?)

➤ Do not mix singular nouns with plural verbs, and vice versa. Example: <The controlling decisions are *Baxter* and *Connolly*.> NOT: <The controlling decision are *Baxter* and *Connolly*.> (In our experience, this particular error is most likely to result from incomplete editing by the writer when the writer suddenly discovers a new case to include in the paragraph. The writer decides to insert a reference to *Connolly*, remembers to change the verb, and then forgets to add an "s" to the word decision.)

CHAPTER 10

Citation and Quotation Basics

Solving legal problems requires applying authority to the facts of the client's case and stating predictive or persuasive propositions. The source of the authority and the support for the propositions are expressed through legal citations. A citation communicates several things to the reader. First, the citation provides the location of the source—where the reader can find the exact source. Second, the citation demonstrates the value of the authority—whether it is primary or secondary, mandatory or persuasive, and whether it supports or contradicts a specific proposition. Third, the citation demonstrates that the lawyer's propositions are well researched, and thus enhances credibility. Finally, the citation provides proper attribution to the words and ideas of others.[1]

---

[1] For an expanded discussion of these purposes, see ALWD & Darby Dickerson, *ALWD Citation Manual: A Professional System of Citation* 3 (3d ed., Aspen Publishers 2005) [hereinafter *ALWD Citation Manual*]. With a few exceptions, the footnotes in this book conform to the *ALWD Citation Manual*.

Citations are a shorthand language, containing words, abbreviations, symbols, and numbers. How well the lawyer "speaks" this language through her citations can affect the reader's perception of the lawyer. A lawyer's poorly written brief, filled with grammatical and punctuation errors, reflects upon the lawyer's credibility and ability—which may ultimately affect the client. The same is true when a lawyer submits a poorly supported brief, filled with incomplete citations or a lack of citations to support specific propositions, or both.

First-year law students are typically taught legal citation through a uniform system, even though practicing lawyers often use citation systems mandated by court rules or state statutes. Most legal writing professors choose to teach legal citation through a uniform system because once students have mastered the basics of citation, they can easily adapt to an individual state's citation rules. The two most common uniform systems are the *ALWD Citation Manual* and *The Bluebook*. The *ALWD Citation Manual* is relatively new and was developed as a "restatement" of citation by the Association of Legal Writing Directors and Dean Darby Dickerson. *The Bluebook* is considerably older and is currently published by the law review students at Harvard University, Yale University, Columbia University, and University of Pennsylvania.[2]

The remainder of this chapter provides general citation rules and basic citation formats for the most commonly cited sources and general rules relating to quotations.[3] This chapter is not a substitute for learning how to use the citation manual that your legal writing professor has assigned. In fact, you

---

[2] For an in-depth discussion of the first edition of the *ALWD Citation Manual* and *The Bluebook: A Uniform System of Citation* (17th ed., Harv. L. Rev. Assn. 2000), including their virtues and shortcomings, see Christine Hurt, *Network Effects and Legal Citation: How Antitrust Theory Predicts Who Will Build a Better Bluebook Mousetrap in the Age of Electronic Mice*, 87 Iowa L. Rev. 1257 (2002). The current version of *The Bluebook* is the 18th edition.

[3] The citation rules follow the *ALWD Citation Manual*, *supra*, n. 1, and *The Bluebook*, 18th edition, released in 2005. Note that the basic components of an *ALWD* citation and a *Bluebook* citation are often the same. However, we will set out specific detailed citations separately in the *ALWD Manual* and *The Bluebook* discussions that follow, so that our reader who uses only one format need not cross-reference back and forth.

will often need your citation manual to look up abbreviations, to understand the more nuanced applications of the basic citation rules discussed below, and to cite sources not covered in this chapter. Do not use these uniform citation formats or follow the examples below if your professor requires that you conform your citations to the local citation rules of a particular jurisdiction.

This chapter is arranged so that the basic citation formats for each system are self-contained. The chapter concludes with basic principles for quoting authority, which are common to both citation systems. If you are learning citation through *The Bluebook*, then skip the next section and go directly to page 122.

ALWD CITATION MANUAL

General Citation Rules

➤ Full and Short Citations

Rule 11 introduces full and short citations. Full citations have a variety of components that provide all the information necessary to locate the source and to determine its relative value. They must be used the first time the source is cited in the document. Short citations have fewer components but still contain sufficient information to locate the source.

Full citation example: *Mendenhall v. Barber-Green Co.*, 531 F. Supp. 951, 954 (N.D. Ill. 1982).

Short citation example: *Mendenhall*, 531 F. Supp. at 954.

The various full-cite and short-cite components of the most commonly cited primary and secondary sources are discussed below.

One short citation format, *id.*, can be used as a short cite with almost any source provided that the *id.* is referring to the immediately preceding authority. If there is an intervening authority cited, then *id.* cannot be used.

➢ Pinpoint References

Rule 5 discusses the need for specific references to the precise page on which the cited source appears, which are known as "pinpoint cites" or "jump cites." Novice legal writers often make the mistake of omitting the pinpoint cites to the precise page. This irritates legal readers. In the example above, both the full and short citation examples contain a pinpoint cite—page 954.

➢ Citation Placement and Use

Rule 43 explains the differences among citation sentences, which are punctuated like a sentence with a period at the end; citation clauses, which are part of a textual sentence separated by commas, unless the clause ends the sentence, requiring a period; and embedded citations, which are a citation incorporated into the sentence as part of the text. Use a citation sentence when the cited source relates to the full textual sentence. Use a citation clause when the cited source relates to part of the sentence. Use an embedded citation when the authority is referenced within the textual sentence.

Citation sentence:
The court rejected the charitable subscription standard in the *Restatement (Second) of Contracts*, stating that to adopt a " 'theory which affords charities a different legal rationale than other entities, is to approve fiction.' " *Mt. Sinai Hosp. v. Jordan*, 290 So. 2d 484, 487 (Fla. 1974) (quoting *Jordan v. Mt. Sinai Hosp.*, 276 So. 2d 102, 108 (Fla. 3d Dist. App. 1973)).

Citation clause:
The Sixth Circuit certified the question to the Michigan Supreme Court, *Frey Dairy v. A. O. Smith Harvestore Prods., Inc.*, 886 F.2d 128, 131 (6th Cir. 1989), but the Michigan Supreme Court declined to address the issue, *Frey Dairy v. A. O. Smith Corp.*, 443 N.W.2d 782, 782 (Mich. 1989).

Embedded citation:
In *Davis v. Findley*, 422 S.E.2d 859, 861 (Ga. 1992), the court held that "a violation of the Code of Professional Responsibility alone could not establish a basis for a negligence action."

On a more subtle level, be cognizant of where you place citations. Try to avoid too many citation clauses or embedded citations. Consider editing the passage if necessary. Additionally, avoid beginning sentences with too many citations. Note, however, an embedded citation sometimes serves as a transition that moves the analysis forward.

➤ Abbreviations

Rule 2 provides a general discussion of using abbreviations for various sources. You will also have to consult the Appendices for the standard abbreviations. Table 9.1 below provides appendices to consult for various sources.

ALWD Citation Manual **Appendices**	
Appendix 1	Primary Sources by Jurisdiction
Appendix 3	General Abbreviations
Appendix 4	Court Abbreviations
Appendix 5	Abbreviations for Legal Periodicals
Appendix 7	Federal Taxation Materials
Appendix 8	Selected Official Federal Administrative Publications

Table 9.1

Tables 9.2 and 9.3 provide abbreviations for the most common federal reporters and for the regional reporters, which, as part of West's National Reporter System, cover primarily the state appellate courts.[4] Table 9.4 provides some of the most commonly used abbreviations for citing to periodicals, cases, and state statutes.

---

[4] The States of California and New York have large populations and high volumes of litigation. Consequently, West established separate reporters for each of these states. These reporters are considered part of West's National Reporter System because they include appellate decisions that do not appear in the regional reporters for those states.

Federal Court	Reporter	Abbreviation
U.S. Supreme Court	United States Reports	U.S.
U.S. Supreme Court	Supreme Court Reporter	S. Ct.
U.S. Supreme Court	United States Supreme Court Reports, Lawyers' Edition	L. Ed. L. Ed. 2d
Courts of Appeal	Federal Reporter	F., F.2d, F.3d
District Courts	Federal Supplement	F. Supp. F. Supp. 2d
District Courts	Federal Rules Decisions	F.R.D.

Table 9.2

Reporter	Abbreviation
Atlantic Reporter	A., A.2d
California Reporter	Cal. Rptr., Cal. Rptr. 2d, Cal. Rptr. 3d
New York Supplement	N.Y.S., N.Y.S.2d
North Eastern Reporter	N.E., N.E.2d
North Western Reporter	N.W., N.W.2d
Pacific Reporter	P., P.2d, P.3d
South Eastern Reporter	S.E., S.E.2d
South Western Reporter	S.W., S.W.2d, S.W.3d
Southern Reporter	So., So. 2d

Table 9.3

Word or Term	Abbreviation
And	&
Annotated	Ann.
Association	Assn.
Bar	B.
Commission	Commn.
Company	Co.
Compilation	Comp.
Corporation	Corp.
Department	Dept.
Incorporated	Inc.
Institute	Inst.
International	Intl.
Journal	J.
Law	L.
Legal	Leg.
Organization	Org.
Review and Revised	Rev.
Statute	Stat.
Transportation	Transp.
United States	U.S.
University	U.

Table 9.4

➢ Capitalization

Rule 3 addresses capitalization. Among the most important rules about capitalization are the following. Capitalize "court" when (1) referring to the United States Supreme Court, but only after the court has been identified by its full name; (2) referring to a state's court of last resort, but only after the court has been identified by its full name; (3) naming any court in full; and (4) referring to the instant court to which the document has been submitted. Capitalize "defendant" and "plaintiff" when referring to the instant litigants—the parties to the litigation that is the subject of the document—and only when submitting that document to a court.

Citing Primary Authority

➢ Constitutions currently in force

Rule 13 covers constitutions. Most frequently, you will cite a constitution currently in force. There are two components to the full citation:

> **Name of constitution**
> **Pinpoint section.**

Use *id.* for the short citation format where appropriate. If *id.* cannot be used, then repeat the full citation.

Full citation to constitution: U.S. Const. art. III, § 1.

Short citation where *id.* is not appropriate: U.S. Const. art. III, § 1.

➢ Statutes currently in force

Rule 14 covers statutory codes, session laws, and slip laws. When citing a statute, cite the official code if available. Otherwise, cite an unofficial code. (If the statute is not published in a code, consult the *ALWD Citation Manual*.) There are five components to a full cite to a federal statute published in an official code:

**Title number
Code abbreviation
Section symbol
Section number
(Date of publication of volume).**

There are six in a full cite to a statute in an unofficial code:

**Title number
Code abbreviation
Section symbol
Section number
(Publisher
Date of publication of volume).**

Full cite to official federal code: 20 U.S.C. § 1001 (2000).

Full cite to unofficial federal code: 20 U.S.C.A. § 1001 (West 2000).
                                                            20 U.S.C.S. § 1001 (Lexis 1999).

(U.S.C.S. is now published by LexisNexis. You may see citations to Lawyers
Cooperative, the former publisher of U.S.C.S.)

For short citations, use *id.* if appropriate. If *id.* cannot be used, then
follow one of the following formats:

Short cite to official federal code: 20 U.S.C. § 1001.
                                                        § 1001.

Short cite to unofficial federal code: 20 U.S.C.A. § 1001.
                                                         § 1001.

                                                       20 U.S.C.S. § 1001.
                                                                   § 1001.

To cite state statutes currently in force, you will have to consult
Appendix 1, Primary Sources by Jurisdiction, to locate the name of the official

(and unofficial, if necessary) statutory codes. The basic components for full and short citations to state codes are similar to those for the federal code. Full citations are often constructed in the following order, although there are variations where the citations to state codes more closely resemble a citation to the federal code.

> **Name of statutory compilation**
> **Section symbol**
> **Section number**
> **([Publisher if applicable] Date of publication of volume).**

Examples of full citations to state statutes:
Utah Code Ann. § 46-4-201 (Lexis 2000).
10 Me. Rev. Stat. Ann. § 9407 (1999).

For short citations, use *id.* if appropriate. If *id.* cannot be used, then follow one of the following formats:

Examples of short citations to state statutes:
Utah Code Ann. § 46-4-201.
                    § 46-4-201.

10 Me. Rev. Stat. Ann. § 9407.
                    § 9407.

In situations where you must cite multiple consecutive sections, separate the sections or subsections with an en dash or the word "to." To cite multiple non-consecutive sections, separate the sections or subsections with a comma. You may also want to consult Rule 6, which addresses citing to sections and paragraphs. To cite a supplement to the main volume, consult Rule 14.

To cite other federal legislative materials, consult *ALWD Citation Manual* Rule 15; for other state legislative materials, consult Rule 16. To cite court rules, ethics rules and opinions, and jury instructions, consult Rule 17. For federal administrative and executive materials, see Rule 19; for state administrative and executive materials, see Rule 20; and for local ordinances, see Rule 18. To cite a U.S. treaty or convention, refer to Rule 21.

➢ Cases

Rule 12 addresses how to cite cases. Although we provide the basic components for full and short citations here, you will have to consult Rule 12 for the many nuances in citing cases where a union, governmental entity, relator, or piece of property is a named party. You should become familiar with two aspects of this rule: First, when an individual is a party, only use the surname in the citation. Second, when an organization is a party, use the full name, but omit abbreviations such as "d/b/a"; if the organization is commonly known by its initials, then you may substitute the initials for the name of the organization; you may abbreviate any word listed of the name included in Appendix 3; and you may delete a second business designation where a name includes two.

A full citation to a case that has no subsequent history has seven components; if the case has a subsequent history—for example the case has been affirmed or reversed—then there are nine components.

> **Case name,**
> **Reporter volume**
> **Reporter abbreviation**
> **Initial page,**
> **Pinpoint page**
> **(Court**
> **Date),**
> **Subsequent history abbreviation [if any],**
> **Subsequent history citation [if any]**.

Full citation without subsequent history:
Georgetown Manor, Inc. v. Ethan Allen, Inc., 753 F. Supp. 936, 939 (S.D. Fla. 1991).

Full citation with subsequent history:
Jordan v. Mt. Sinai Hosp. of Greater Miami, Inc., 276 So. 2d 102, 105 (Fla. 3d Dist. App. 1973), *aff'd*, 290 So. 2d 484 (Fla. 1974).

There are three ways to provide a short citation to a case. First, use *id.* if appropriate. Second, if the case name is not included in the textual sentence (of the memorandum, client letter, or brief), then include the following components:

Name of one party,
Volume number
Reporter abbreviation
at
Pinpoint page.

Third, if the case name is part of the textual sentence, then include the following components:

Volume number
Reporter abbreviation
at
Pinpoint page.

Short citation where case name is not included in textual sentence:
MCI Commun., 708 F.2d at 1084.

Short citation where case name is included in textual sentence:
708 F.2d at 1084.

When citing to a plurality, concurring, or dissenting opinion, you must provide a parenthetical that identifies the source as a non-majority opinion. If you are citing a plurality opinion, then merely note "plurality" in the parenthetical. If you are citing a concurring or dissenting opinion, then provide the last name of each judge who participated in the concurring or dissenting opinion and his or her official designation (usually J. for judge or justice; JJ. for judges or justices), followed by the type of minority opinion. This rule applies to full and all short citations.

Full citation denoting dissenting opinion:
Howard v. Babcock, 863 P.2d 150, 161 (Cal. 1993) (Kennard, J., dissenting).

Short citation:
Howard, 863 P.2d at 161 (Kennard, J., dissenting).

In some situations, you may have to provide a parallel citation, which is a citation to another source or sources that have published the exact same authority. For example, it is not uncommon for a state to have an official reporter, published by the state, and an unofficial reporter, often published by West. Thus, an appellate opinion from that state will be published in at least two reporters. Some local court rules require citations to all the sources. Consult *ALWD Citation Manual* Appendix 2 to determine whether a document submitted to a particular court requires parallel citations. In a parallel citation, the court abbreviation is not provided in the parenthetical because the official reporter identifies the court. Appendix 1 provides a listing of each state's court system and reporters.

Parallel Citations:
Estate of Timko v. Oral Roberts Evangelistic Assn., 51 Mich. App. 662, 215 N.W.2d 750 (1974).

Waters v. Union Trust Co., 129 Mich. 640, 89 N.W. 687 (1902).

To determine how to cite cases not yet reported, cases that are unreported, and cases published on the Internet, consult Rule 12.

Citing Secondary Authority

➢ Restatements

Rule 27 provides the citation format for Restatements, as well as model codes, uniform laws, and sentencing guidelines. There are four components to a full citation for a Restatement:

Title
Section symbol
Pinpoint section
(Date of publication).

For short citations, use *id.* if appropriate. If *id.* cannot be used, then omit the date parenthetical.

Full citation: *Restatement (Second) of Contracts* § 90 (1981)

Short citation: *Restatement (Second) of Contracts* §§ 24–34.

➤ **Legal Periodicals (Law Reviews)**

Rule 23 covers citation formats for legal and other periodicals. The basic full citation to a law review article has seven components:

> **Author,**
> **Title,**
> **Volume number**
> **Periodical abbreviation**
> **Initial page,**
> **Pinpoint page**
> **(Date).**

There are some nuances to this rule, especially regarding authors. If there are two authors, provide the full name of each, separated by an ampersand. If there are more than two authors, then you may use the term "et al." following the first author's name. If the author is a student, then include the designation "Student Author" after the student's name. To locate the periodical abbreviation, consult Appendix 5.

Article with one author:
Charles L. Knapp, *Reliance in the Revised Restatement: The Proliferation of Promissory Estoppel*, 81 Colum. L. Rev. 52, 60 (1981).

Article with more than two authors:
Mary Francis Budig et al., *Pledges to Nonprofit Organizations: Are They Enforceable and Must They Be Enforced?*, 27 U.S.F. L. Rev. 47, 68–69 (1992).

Article by student author:
Glenn S. Draper, Student Author, *Enforcing Covenants Not to Compete*, 69 Wash. L. Rev. 161, 162 (1994).

For short citations to legal periodicals, use *id.*, if appropriate. If *id.* cannot be used, then provide the following components:

Author's last name,
Volume number
Periodical abbreviation
at
Pinpoint page.

Short citation formats: Knapp, 81 Colum. L. Rev. at 55.

Budig et al., 27 U.S.F. L. Rev. at 50.

Draper, 69 Wash. L. Rev. at 169.

To cite symposia, colloquia, survey and special issues, multipart articles, newspapers, newsletters, and electronic journals, consult Rule 23.

➤ Books

Rule 22 demonstrates how to cite books, treatises, and nonperiodic materials. A full citation to a book or treatise typically contains the following components:

Author,
Title
Pinpoint section and/or page

**(Editor [if any],
Edition [if any],
Publisher
Date).**

Full citation to book with two authors:
James J. White & Robert S. Summers, *Uniform Commercial Code* § 10-4, 375–77 (4th ed., West 1995).

Full citation to a book with an editor:
Oliver Wendell Holmes, *The Common Law* 195 (Mark DeWolfe Howe ed., Little, Brown & Co. 1963).

For short citations to books and treatises, use *id.*, if appropriate. If *id.* cannot be used, then provide the following components:

Author's last name,
Title
at
Pinpoint section and/or page.

Short citation: White & Summers, *Uniform Commercial Code* at § 6-5, 210.

Holmes, *The Common Law* at 209.

To cite books and treatises with organizational authors, works in a series, collected works of one author, and collected works of several authors, see Rule 22.

Working with Signals

Rule 44 addresses signals. Signals are used as part of a citation to authority to explain the type and degree of support (or contradiction) that the source cited provides. They are very common in law review articles. When using a signal, explanatory parentheticals, which are covered in Rule 46, are highly encouraged. Do not use a signal if the authority directly supports the stated proposition. In writing office memoranda, client letters, and briefs, use signals sparingly. Table 9.5 provides those signals that would most likely be used in legal documents.

Signal	Use in these situations
E.g.	The cited authority is representative or an example of other authorities not listed that stand for the same textual proposition. *E.g.* can be combined with other signals.
See	The cited authority (a) implicitly supports or (b) contains dicta that support the stated textual proposition.
See also	The cited authority supports the stated textual proposition, but not as directly or strongly as when no signal or "see" is used.
Contra	The cited authority directly contradicts the stated textual proposition.
But see	The cited authority (a) implicitly contradicts or (b) contains dictum that contradicts the stated textual proposition.
See generally	The cited authority provides helpful background information relating to the stated textual proposition.

Table 9.5

To determine the order of signals and when to repeat signals, consult Rule 44. To determine how to cite several sources within the same signal, consult Rule 45.

If you are learning citation through the *ALWD Manual* only, proceed to page 137 for a discussion of quotation principles.

THE BLUEBOOK

In working with *The Bluebook*, it is important to recognize that *The Bluebook's* authors have designated different typefaces for different types of documents. For court documents and legal memoranda, ordinary type and italics are used. For law review articles, three are used: ordinary roman, italics, and large and small capitals. You will not use large and small capitals in your legal memoranda and court documents. The basics of *Bluebook* citing to court documents and legal memoranda are provided in the Bluepages of *The Bluebook*, but in determining how to cite certain authorities, you will often have to convert rules applicable to law review style to practitioner style.

General Citation Rules

> #### Full and Short Citations

Full citations, which have a variety of components that provide all the information necessary to locate the source and to determine its relative value, must be used the first time the source is cited in the document. Short citations have fewer components but still contain sufficient information to locate the source.

Full citation example:	*Mendenhall v. Barber-Green Co.*, 531 F. Supp. 951, 954 (N.D. Ill. 1982).
Short citation example:	*Mendenhall*, 531 F. Supp. at 954.

The various full-cite and short-cite components of the most commonly cited primary and secondary sources are discussed below.

One short citation format, *id.*, can be used as a short cite with any source provided that the *id.* is referring to the immediately preceding authority. If there is an intervening authority cited, then *id.* cannot be used.

> ## Pinpoint References

The Bluebook requires specific references to the precise page on which the cited source appears, which are known as "pinpoint cites" or "jump cites." Novice legal writers often make the mistake of omitting the pinpoint cites to the precise page. This irritates legal readers. In the example above, both the full and short citation examples contain a pinpoint cite—page 954.

> ## Citation Placement and Use

Bluepages B2 explains the difference between a citation sentence, which is punctuated like a sentence with a period at the end, and a citation clause, which is part of a textual sentence separated by commas, unless the clause ends the sentence, requiring a period. Use a citation sentence when the cited source relates to the full textual sentence. Use a citation clause when the cited source relates to part of the sentence.

Citation sentence:
The court rejected the charitable subscription standard in the *Restatement (Second) of Contracts*, stating that to adopt a " 'theory which affords charities a different legal rationale than other entities, is to approve fiction.' " *Mount Sinai Hosp. v. Jordan*, 290 So. 2d 484, 487 (Fla. 1974) (quoting *Jordan v. Mount Sinai Hosp.*, 276 So. 2d 102, 108 (Fla. Dist. Ct. App. 1973)).

Citation clauses:
The Sixth Circuit certified the question to the Michigan Supreme Court, *Frey Dairy v. A. O. Smith Harvestore Products, Inc.*, 886 F.2d 128, 131 (6th Cir. 1989), but the Michigan Supreme Court declined to address the issue, *Frey Dairy v. A. O. Smith Corp.*, 443 N.W.2d 782, 782 (Mich. 1989).

On a more subtle level, be cognizant of where you place citations. Try to avoid too many citation clauses. Consider editing the passage if necessary. Additionally, avoid beginning a sentence with a citation. But note, introducing a case sometimes provides a transition, which moves the analysis forward.

➢ **Abbreviations**

Rule 6 requires the use of abbreviations listed in the tables provided at the end of *The Bluebook*, which you will have to consult. Table 9.6 below provides a list of the tables to consult to locate the abbreviations for various sources.

The Bluebook **Tables**	
Table 1	United States Jurisdictions
Table 2	Foreign Jurisdictions
Table 3	Intergovernmental Organizations
Table 4	Treaty Sources
Table 5	Arbitral Reporters
Table 6	Case Names
Table 7	Court Names
Table 8	Explanatory Phrases
Table 9	Legislative Documents
Table 10	Geographical Terms
Table 11	Judges and Officials
Table 12	Months
Table 13	Periodicals
Table 14	Publishing Terms
Table 15	Services
Table 16	Subdivisions

Table 9.6

Tables 9.7 and 9.8 provide abbreviations for the most common federal reporters and for the regional reporters, which, as part of West's National Reporter System, cover primarily the state appellate courts. Table 9.9 provides some of the most commonly used abbreviations for citing to periodicals, cases, and state statutes.

Federal Court	Reporter	Abbreviation
U.S. Supreme Court	United States Reports	U.S.
U.S. Supreme Court	Supreme Court Reporter	S. Ct.
U.S. Supreme Court	United States Supreme Court Reports, Lawyers' Edition	L. Ed. L. Ed. 2d
Courts of Appeal	Federal Reporter	F., F.2d, F.3d
District Courts	Federal Supplement	F. Supp. F. Supp. 2d
District Courts	Federal Rules Decisions	F.R.D.

Table 9.7

Reporter	Abbreviation
Atlantic Reporter	A., A.2d
California Reporter	Cal. Rptr., Cal. Rptr. 2d, Cal. Rptr. 3d
New York Supplement	N.Y.S., N.Y.S.2d
North Eastern Reporter	N.E., N.E.2d
North Western Reporter	N.W., N.W.2d
Pacific Reporter	P., P.2d, P.3d
South Eastern Reporter	S.E., S.E.2d
South Western Reporter	S.W., S.W.2d, S.W.3d
Southern Reporter	So., So. 2d

Table 9.8

Word or Term	Abbreviation
And	&
Annotated	Ann.
Association	Ass'n
Bar	B.
Commission	Comm'n
Company	Co.
Compilation	Comp.
Corporation	Corp.
Department	Dep't
Incorporated	Inc.
Institute	Inst.
International	Int'l
Journal	J.
Law	L.
Legal	Legal
Organization	Org.
Review and Revised	Rev.
Statute	Stat.
Transportation	Transp.
United States	U.S. (but not where the United States is a party.
University	U. (periodicals and books) Univ. (case names)

Table 9.9

➢ Capitalization

Bluepages B10.6.1 states that in court documents and legal memoranda, the following capitalization norms must be followed. First, capitalize "Court" when referring to the U.S. Supreme Court, when naming a court in full, and when referring to the court that will receive the document.

Second, capitalize to denote the instant parties' designations—those parties who are the subject of the memorandum or court document. These include Plaintiff, Defendant, Appellant, and Appellee. (Of course, it is perfectly acceptable to use proper names as well.) Third, capitalize the specific titles of those court documents that have been filed in the case that is the subject of the legal memorandum or court document. (You may also need to consult Rule 8.)

Citing Primary Authority

➢ Constitutions currently in force

Rule 11 covers constitutions. Most frequently, you will cite a constitution currently in force. There are two components to the full citation:

Name of constitution
Pinpoint section.

Use _id._ for the short citation format where appropriate. If _id._ cannot be used, then repeat the full citation.

Full citation to constitution: U.S. Const. art. III, § 1.

Short citation where _id._ is not appropriate: U.S. Const. art. III, § 1.

➤ Statutes currently in force

Rule 12 covers statutory codes, session laws, and slip laws. When citing to a statute, cite the official code if available. Otherwise, cite an unofficial code. (If the statute is not published in a code, consult *The Bluebook*.) There are five components to a full cite to a federal statute published in an official code:

Title number
Code abbreviation
Section symbol
Section number
(Date of publication that appears on the spine, the title page, or the latest copyright year, in that order of preference).

There are six in a full cite to a statute in an unofficial code:

Title number
Code abbreviation
Section symbol
Section number
(Publisher
Date of publication that appears on the spine, the title page, or the latest copyright year, in that order of preference).

Full cite to official federal code: 20 U.S.C. § 1001 (2000).

Full cite to unofficial federal code: 20 U.S.C.A. § 1001 (West 2000).
                                                            20 U.S.C.S. § 1001 (LEXIS 1999).

(U.S.C.S. is now published by LexisNexis. You may see citations to Lawyers Cooperative, the former publisher of U.S.C.S.)

For short citations, use *id.* if appropriate. If *id.* cannot be used, then provide the following components:

Short cite to official federal code:	20 U.S.C. § 1001.
Short cite to unofficial federal code:	20 U.S.C.A. § 1001. 20 U.S.C.S. § 1001.

To cite state statutes currently in force, you will have to consult Table 1 to locate the name of the official (and unofficial, if necessary) statutory codes. The basic components for full and short citations to state codes are similar to those for the federal code. Full citations are typically constructed in the following order, although there are variations where the citations to state codes more closely resemble a citation to the federal code:

Name of statutory compilation
Section symbol
Section number
([Publisher if applicable] Date of publication that appears on the spine, the title page, or the latest copyright year, in that order of preference).

Examples of full citations to state statutes:
Utah Code Ann. § 46-6-53 (1998).
Me. Rev. Stat. Ann. tit. 10, § 1474 (West 1997).

For short citations, use *id.* if appropriate. If *id.* cannot be used, then provide all the components except the date.

In situations where you must cite multiple consecutive sections, separate the sections or subsections with an en dash. To cite multiple non-consecutive sections, separate the sections or subsections with a comma. You may also want to consult Rule 3. To cite a supplement to the main volume, consult Rules 12 and 3.

To cite other legislative materials, consult *Bluebook* Rule 13. To cite Rules of Court, Procedure, Evidence, and Ethics, consult Rule 12. For administrative and executive materials, consult Rule 14.

> ## Cases

Rule 10 covers how to cite cases. Although we provide the basic components for full and short citations here, you will have to consult Rule 10 for the many nuances in citing cases where a union, governmental entity, realtor, or piece of property is a named party; and you will need to consult Tables 1, 6, 7, 8, 10, and 11 to locate the appropriate abbreviations.

A full citation to a case that has no subsequent history has seven components; if the case has a subsequent history—for example the case has been affirmed or reversed—then there are nine components.

> *Case name*,
> **Reporter volume**
> **Reporter abbreviation**
> **Initial page**,
> **Pinpoint page**
> **(Court**
> **Date)**,
> *Subsequent history abbreviation* **[if any]**,
> **subsequent history citation [if any]**.

Full citation without subsequent history:
Georgetown Manor, Inc. v. Ethan Allen, Inc., 753 F. Supp. 936, 939 (S.D. Fla. 1991).

Full citation with subsequent history:
Jordan v. Mt. Sinai Hosp. of Greater Miami, Inc., 276 So. 2d 102, 105 (Fla. Dist. Ct. App. 1973), *aff'd*, 290 So. 2d 484 (Fla. 1974).

There are three ways to provide a short citation to a case. First, use *id.* if appropriate. Second, if the case name is not included in the textual sentence (of the memorandum, client letter, or brief), then include the following components:

> **Name of one party,**
> **Volume number**
> **Reporter abbreviation**
> **at**
> **Pinpoint page.**

Third, if the case name is part of the textual sentence, then you may include only the following components:

> **Volume number**
> **Reporter abbreviation**
> **at**
> **Pinpoint page.**

Short citation where case name is not included in textual sentence:
MCI Communications, 708 F.2d at 1084.

Short citation where case name is included in textual sentence:
708 F.2d at 1084.

When citing to a plurality, concurring, or dissenting opinion, you must provide a parenthetical that identifies the source as a non-majority opinion. If you are citing a plurality opinion, then merely note "plurality" in the parenthetical. If you are citing a concurring or dissenting opinion, then provide the last name of each judge who participated in the concurring or dissenting opinion and his or her official designation (usually J. for judge or justice; JJ. for judges or justices), followed by the type of minority opinion. This rule applies to full and all short citations.

Full citation denoting dissenting opinion:
Howard v. Babcock, 863 P.2d 150, 161 (Cal. 1993) (Kennard, J., dissenting).

Short citation:
Howard, 863 P.2d at 161 (Kennard, J., dissenting).

In some situations, you may have to provide a parallel citation, which is a citation to another source or sources that have published the exact same authority. For example, it is not uncommon for a state to have an official reporter, published by the state, and an unofficial reporter, often published by West. Thus, an appellate opinion from that state will be published in at least two reporters. Some local court rules require citations to all the sources. Consult the state's local court rules to determine whether a document submitted to a court in that state requires parallel citations. In a parallel citation, the court abbreviation is not provided in the parenthetical because the official reporter identifies the court. Table 1 provides a listing of each state's court system and reporters.

Parallel Citations:

Estate of Timko v. Oral Roberts Evangelistic Ass'n, 51 Mich. Ct. App. 662, 215 N.W.2d 750 (1974).

Waters v. Union Trust Co., 129 Mich. 640, 89 N.W. 687 (1902).

To determine how to cite cases not yet reported, cases that are unreported, and cases published on the Internet, consult Rules 10 and 18.

Citing Secondary Authority

➢ **Restatements**

Rule 12 provides the citation format for Restatements, as well as model codes, standards, and sentencing guidelines. There are four components to a full citation for a Restatement:

> **Title**
> **Section symbol**
> **Pinpoint section**
> **(Date).**

For short citations, use *id.* if appropriate. If *id.* cannot be used, then omit the date parenthetical.

Full citation: Restatement (Second) of Contracts § 90 (1981).

> **Short citation:** Restatement (Second) of Contracts §§ 24–34.

➢ Legal Periodicals (Law Reviews)

Rule 16 covers citation formats for legal and other periodicals. The basic full citation to a law review article has seven components:

Author,
Title,
Volume number
Periodical abbreviation
Initial page,
Pinpoint page
(Date).

There are some nuances to this rule, especially regarding authors. If there are two authors, provide the full name of each, separated by an ampersand. If there are more than two authors, then use the term "et al." following the first author's name. If the author is a student, then include the designation "Note" or "Comment" (depending on the type of article) after the student's name. To locate the periodical abbreviation, consult Table 13.

Article with one author:
Charles L. Knapp, *Reliance in the Revised Restatement: The Proliferation of Promissory Estoppel*, 81 Colum. L. Rev. 52, 60 (1981).

Article with more than two authors:
Mary Francis Budig et al., *Pledges to Nonprofit Organizations: Are They Enforceable and Must They Be Enforced?*, 27 U.S.F. L. Rev. 47, 68–69 (1992).

Article by student author:
Glenn S. Draper, Comment, *Enforcing Covenants Not to Compete*, 69 Wash. L. Rev. 161, 162 (1994).

For short citations to legal periodicals, use *id.*, if appropriate. If *id.* cannot be used, then provide the following components:

Author's last name,
supra,
at
Pinpoint page.

Short citation formats: Knapp, *supra*, at 55. Budig et al., *supra*, at 50. Draper, *supra*, at 169.

To cite symposia, colloquia, survey and special issues, multipart articles, magazines, newspapers, newsletters, annotations, and proceedings by institutes and ABA sections, consult Rule 16.

➢ Books

Rule 15 demonstrates how to cite books, pamphlets, and non-periodic materials. A full citation to a book or treatise typically contains the following components:

Author,
Title
Pinpoint section and/or page
(Editor [if any],
Edition [if any],
Date).

Full citation to book with two authors: James J. White & Robert S. Summers, *Uniform Commercial Code* § 10-4, 375–77 (4th ed., 1995).

Full citation to a book with an editor:

Oliver Wendell Holmes, *The Common Law* 195 (Mark DeWolfe Howe ed., 1963).

For short citations to books and treatises, use *id.*, if appropriate. If *id.* cannot be used, then provide the following components:

Author's last name,
***supra*,**
at
Pinpoint section and/or page.

Short citation: White & Summers, *supra*, at § 6-5, 210.

Holmes, *supra*, at 209.

To cite books and treatises with organizational authors, works in a series, collected works of one author, and collected works of several authors, see Rule 15.

Working with Signals

Rule 1 addresses signals. Signals are used as part of a citation to authority to explain the type and degree of support (or contradiction) that the source cited provides. They are extremely common in law review articles. When using a signal, explanatory parentheticals, which are covered in Rule 1 (at 1.5), are highly encouraged. Do not use a signal if the authority directly supports the stated proposition. In writing office memoranda, briefs, and client letters, use signals sparingly. Table 9.10 provides those signals that would most likely be used in legal documents.

Signal	Use in these situations
E.g.,	The cited authority is representative or an example of other authorities not listed that stand for the same textual proposition. *E.g.* can be combined with other signals.
See	The cited authority clearly supports the stated proposition inferentially, requiring the reader to link the cited authority and the textual proposition.
Accord	Where the preceding cited authority directly supports the stated proposition, then *accord* introduces additional cases not named or cited in the textual proposition.
See also	The cited authority provides additional support for the stated textual proposition.[5]
Contra	The cited authority directly contradicts the stated textual proposition. (*Contra* is used the same way that no signal is used for support.)
But see	The cited authority clearly contradicts the stated textual proposition inferentially. (*But see* is used in the same way that *see* would be used for support.)
See generally	The cited authority provides helpful background information relating to the stated textual proposition.

Table 9.10

To determine the order of signals, consult Rule 1.3. To determine how to cite several sources within the same signal, consult Rule 1.4.

---

[5] For a good discussion on the complexity involved in discerning the subtleties among the signals "see," "accord," and "see also," see Calleros, *supra* ch. 7 n. 2, at 297-300.

GENERAL RULES ON QUOTING AUTHORITY

Both the *ALWD Citation Manual* (Rules 47–49) and *The Bluebook* (Rule 5) provide the mechanics of proper quotation format, which includes when and how to provide a block quotation; how to properly indicate alterations and omissions from the original source; and how to indicate the proper paragraph structure when more than one paragraph is quoted.

➤ Block Quotations

A direct quotation of fifty or more words should be block quoted by indenting the right and left margins and using single space. The *ALWD Citation Manual* also suggests block-quoting text that exceeds four lines.

Do not set off the block quotation by quotation marks. Only use quotation marks internally to denote a quotation within a quotation. Provide the citation at the left margin, one double space below the end of the block quote. More important, limit your use of block quotations. Use them to quote long statutory sections or an especially important passage from a case or secondary source.

Example of a block quotation:

Under Michigan's enactment of the Uniform Electronic Transactions Act,

> (1) An electronic record or electronic signature is attributable to a person if it is the act of the person. The act of the person may be shown in any manner, including a showing of the efficacy of any security procedure applied to determine the person to which the electronic record or electronic signature was attributable. (2) The effect of an electronic record or electronic signature attributed to a person under subsection (1) is determined from the context and surrounding circumstances at the time of its creation, execution, or adoption, including any agreements of the parties, and otherwise as provided by law.

Mich. Comp. Laws Ann. § 450.839 (West 2000).

➢ Shorter Quotations

Quotations of fewer than fifty words should be enclosed in quotation marks and integrated within the body of the text of the document. If the cited authority is quoting another source, that passage is set off by single quotation marks. Commas and periods always appear inside the quotation marks. Other punctuation marks appear within the quote only if they are part of the original text. In court documents and legal memoranda, place the citation to the quote immediately after the quoted passage.

Example of a shorter quotation:

The court reaffirmed its previous holdings that the mutual promises between subscribers of pledges for a lawful purpose are enforceable. *Congregation B'Nai Sholom v. Martin*, 173 N.W.2d 504, 510 (Mich. 1969). The court reasoned that the doctrine reflects the sound public policy that one who has " 'voluntarily made a valid and binding subscription to a charity of his choice should not be permitted to evade it.' " *Id.* (quoting *More Game Birds in Am. v. Boettinger*, 14 A.2d 778, 780 (N.J. 1940)).

➢ Alterations and Omissions

Brackets are used to demonstrate alterations such as when a letter is changed from upper to lower case, or vice versa. Similarly, brackets are used to denote inserted material and substituted words or letters.

Original:
We disagree with the Collection's contention that the words expressed on the pledge form are sufficient to make promises of donations legally binding.

Alteration:
The court "disagree[d] with the [charity's] contention that the words ['I welcome the privilege of subscribing'] expressed on the pledge form [were] sufficient to make [the] promise[] of [a] donation[] legally binding."

This is an extreme example of altering the text. As you can see, the symbols to denote the alterations interfere with ease of reading. In this example, changing the plural forms to singular is not necessary. The verb changes were necessary; and the substituted and inserted words help to clarify the meaning. However, in making any alteration, ask if it is even necessary to use a quotation. (Constitutional provisions, statutes, and administrative and court rules must be quoted.) Consider the following revision based on the above example.

Revision:
The charity claimed that the words "I welcome the privilege of subscribing" were sufficient to make the pledge enforceable. [Insert citation.] The court disagreed.

Ellipses are used to indicate omissions in the original text. An ellipsis is three periods, each separated by a space (. . .).   Do not use an ellipsis in the following situations: when quoting a phrase or a clause, when beginning a quotation, and when omitting footnotes or citations.   Do use ellipses to indicate the omission of words or sentences from the middle of the quoted material. There are two examples provided below. The first is based on an edited version of the statute quoted above. The second is based on original text from a case.

Original:

(1) An electronic record or electronic signature is attributable to a person if it is the act of the person. The act of the person may be shown in any manner, including a showing of the efficacy of any security procedure applied to determine the person to which the electronic record or electronic signature was attributable.

(2) The effect of an electronic record or electronic signature attributed to a person under subsection (1) is determined from the context and surrounding circumstances at the time of its creation, execution, or adoption, including any agreements of the parties, and otherwise as provided by law.

Mich. Comp. Laws Ann. § 450.839 (West 2000).

Quote with omissions:

Under Michigan's enactment of the Uniform Electronic Transactions Act, "[a]n . . . electronic signature is attributable to a person if it is the act of the person. The act of the person may be shown in any manner . . . ."   Mich. Comp. Laws Ann. § 450.839(1) (West 2000).

Original:

(from *Thomas v. Bethea*, 718 A.2d 1187, 1194–95 (Md. 1998) downloaded verbatim from Westlaw)

The principle that a lawyer may be held liable for negligence in the handling of a case that was ultimately settled by the client, whether based on deficiencies in preparation that prejudiced the case and more or less required a settlement or on a negligent evaluation of the client's case, has been accepted by nearly every court that has faced the issue. In addition to the cases cited above, *see Edmondson v. Dressman*, 469 So. 2d 571 (Ala.1985); *Callahan v. Clark*, 321 Ark. 376, 901 S.W.2d 842 (1995); *Bill Branch Chev. v. Philip L. Burnett*, 555 So. 2d 455 (Fla. Dist. Ct. App. 1990); *McCarthy v. Pedersen & Houpt*, 250 Ill. App. 3d 166, 190 Ill. Dec. 228, 621 N.E.2d 97 (1993); *Braud v. New England Ins. Co.*, 534 So. 2d 13 (La. Ct. App.1988); *Fishman v. Brooks*, *supra*, 396 Mass. 643, 487 N.E.2d 1377 (1986); *Lowman v. Karp*, *supra*, 190 Mich. Ct. App. at 448, 476 N.W.2d at 428; *Cook v. Connolly*, 366 N.W.2d 287 (Minn.1985); *Bruning v. Law Offices of Palagi, P.C.*, 250 Neb. 677, 551 N.W.2d 266 (1996); *Malfabon v. Garcia*, *supra*, 111 Nev. at 793, 898 P.2d at 107; *Rodriguez v. Horton*, 95 N.M. 356, 622 P.2d 261 (App. 1980); *Becker v. Julien, Blitz & Schlesinger*, 95 Misc. 2d 64, 406 N.Y.S.2d 412 (Sup. 1977); [FN5] *DePugh v. Sladoje*, 111 Ohio App. 3d 675, 676 N.E.2d 1231, 1239 (1996); *Crowley v. Harvey & Battey*, 327 S.C. 68, 488 S.E.2d 334 (1997); *Helmbrecht v. St. Paul Ins. Co.*, 122 Wis. 2d 94, 362 N.W.2d 118 (1985); *Hipwell By and Through Jensen v. Sharp*, 858 P.2d 987 (Utah 1993).

Quote with omissions, using a short citation form:

The *Thomas* court further explained that "[t]he principle that a lawyer may be held liable for negligence in the handling of a case that was ultimately settled by the client, whether based on [poor] preparation . . . or on a negligent evaluation . . . , has been accepted by nearly every court that has faced the issue." 718 A.2d at 1194-95 (citations and footnotes omitted).

Alterations and omissions can be very useful when incorporating quotations; but quotes should be used sparingly. Novice legal writers often include too many quotations in their legal memoranda and briefs. Be judicious in using quotes and saintly in editing them: Never distort the original meaning.

COMMON QUESTIONS ABOUT WHEN AND WHAT TO CITE

The bulk of this chapter has been devoted to *how* to cite, but there are five related questions that frequently surface about *when* and *what* to cite. We will cover them because they commonly plague legal writers.

Question: When do I have to cite authority?

Answer: Remember that citing authority provides support for your predictions and arguments. Our advice is to follow the rules provided in the materials created by the Legal Writing Institute. Provide a citation when:

➢ Directly using another's words;

➢ Paraphrasing another's words;

➢ Directly using another's idea; and

➢ Building upon the analysis or sources of another.[6]

Question: What do I do when I find a recent case that in turn cites an older case as support for a legal principle? Do I cite the recent case? Do I cite the older case? Do I cite both?

Answer: It depends. All other things being equal, you rely on recent cases rather than older ones. But everything is not always equal. Sometimes the older case is from a higher court than the recent case. Sometimes the older case is a landmark. Sometimes you want your audience to understand that the

---

[6] For a more in-depth explanation of attribution, including examples, see the Legal Writing Institute's website <www.lwionline.org> (link to the Institute's Plagiarism Brochure).

legal principle is venerable. Sometimes one of the cases is binding authority in your jurisdiction, while the other is from a court whose opinions are only persuasive authority. Here are our rules of thumb:

> ➤ If (a) you are only going to cite one case, and (b) the two opinions are from the same court, then cite the most recent opinion.

> ➤ If (a) you are only going to cite one case, (b) the two opinions are from different courts, and (c) the opinions of both courts are binding in your jurisdiction (e.g., one of the opinions is from your state's supreme court and the other opinion is from your state's intermediate court of appeals), then cite the higher court.

> ➤ If (a) you are only going to cite one case, (b) the two opinions are from different courts, and (c) one opinion is binding authority in your jurisdiction while the other is from a court whose opinions are merely persuasive authority, then cite the binding authority.

> ➤ If (a) you are only going to cite one case, (b) the two opinions are from different courts, and (c) neither opinion is binding in your jurisdiction, then cite the higher court first. If they are courts of equal rank (e.g., both are state supreme courts,) then cite the most recent opinion.

> ➤ When in doubt, cite both cases. If you are going to cite both, then follow the above rules of thumb in deciding which case to list first, and put in a descriptor for the second case: *Doe v. Roe*, XX F. Supp. 2d 25, 29 (D. Minn. 20XX) (citing *Jones v. Wombat*, XX F. Supp. 45, 49 (D. Minn. 20XX)). If the *Roe* case quoted from the *Wombat* case, then you would say "quoting from" in place of "citing."

Question: What do I do when I find two cases, and the more recent one refers to the older one, but they do not stand for exactly the same legal principle?

Answer: In that setting, our rule of thumb is to cite the case that most directly fits your own legal problem. Then, if you wish, you may refer to the other case, with an appropriate parenthetical descriptor: *Doe v. Roe*, XX F. Supp. 2d 25, 29 (D. Minn. 20XX) (extending *Jones v. Wombat*, XX F. Supp. 45, 49 (D. Minn. 20XX)). Other descriptors might include "distinguishing," "relying upon," "expanding upon," and the like.

Question: How do I know when I have cited enough authority to support a legal principle?

Answer: It depends. One great statute or case directly on point and binding in your jurisdiction may be sufficient. You present that statute or case in detail, explain why it is controlling, and get out.

But there may not be a great statute or case directly on point. If there is not, then you have to cite enough authority to be able to *synthesize a pattern* in the case law, sometimes from another jurisdiction, that resolves the problem you are addressing.

Question: What if I have cited an authority once in a particular discussion paragraph. Do I have to keep citing the same authority all the time in the same discussion?

Answer: It depends. A simple example will illustrate the point: One of the authors once had a discussion with a student teaching assistant over whether every sentence in an office memorandum she was reviewing should contain a citation to underlying source material. The TA thought there should be. The author thought not. The logic of the TA, a law review editor, was that the reader should have a cite to every thought to enable the reader to do research and to take comfort in the accuracy of the analysis. The logic of the author was that the piece was an office memo for a hypothetical colleague and a client. Neither of those hypothetical audience members was likely to conduct independent follow-up research. Both audience members likely assumed accuracy. Both mostly wanted an easily readable piece with a quick bottom-line conclusion. Thus, in context, occasional cites were important to establish a basis for the opinion, but cites to every thought just interrupted the flow of the document. The author and the TA explained the difference of opinion to the class and told the students they could make a reasonable professional judgment of their own.

CHAPTER 11

Communicating a Predictive Analysis

Up until now, we have provided the fundamental building blocks for legal analysis and communication. In the last two chapters of this book, we will discuss how to put everything together in the context of preparing four types of legal documents: two predictive forms, office memoranda and client advice letters; and two persuasive forms, trial court briefs and appellate briefs.[1] In other words, the focus is now on the actual presentation of your problem-solving efforts. This chapter provides common features of office memoranda and client advice letters and a sample of each. By providing these samples, however, we do not intend to suggest that these are the only ways to present a predictive analysis.

---

[1] There are, of course, many other types of legal documents. We only address those that are most frequently the subject of first-year legal writing courses. The principles described in this book, however, often will be relevant to other types of legal documents.

COMMON FEATURES OF GOOD PREDICTIVE WRITING

   1. In either an office memorandum for a colleague or client, or an advice letter for a client, use some version of the IRAC template. Most, if not all, office memoranda and client advice letters do the following: identify the problem to be addressed, present the legal rule that will govern the problem, explain the rule, apply the rule to the specific facts of the problem, and formulate a conclusion that predicts how the law will resolve the problem. Client advice letters may additionally provide recommendations.

   2. Offer a solution to a problem. Lawyers are in the problem-solving business. Colleagues and clients do not want mere interesting discussions. They want to know how the law will likely apply to a specific problem. Give them an answer. If you need to qualify it with "likely," "maybe," "unlikely," or some other descriptor that hedges your answer for malpractice or other purposes, then fine. But you still have to give an answer. "Gee, this is a hard one," is not acceptable. If the questions were easy, you would not be needed.

   3. Try to find a favorable solution to the problem, and if you have to say no, then look for ways to soften the blow. Colleagues and clients do not really want to hear why the law *will not let them* do something they want to do, or alternatively, why the law *will let an adversary* do something they do not want the adversary to do. They want you to give them favorable solutions. Try to do that. Do not give them unfavorable answers without first digging hard, really hard, for favorable ones.

   Recognize, however, that sometimes your answer must be no. Sometimes the law simply prohibits your client from doing something. Sometimes ethical constraints prevent you from recommending a particular course of action. And then there are also the circumstances covered by a famous quote from a former United States Secretary of State, Elihu Root, who is reported to have said that " '[a]bout half of the practice of a decent lawyer is telling would-be clients that they are damned fools and should stop.' "[2]

---

   [2] *McCandless v. Great A. & P. Tea Co.*, 697 F.2d 198, 201-02 (7th Cir. 1983) (quoting A. Kaufman, *Problems in Professional Responsibility* (1976)).

This does not mean that you should relish saying no to a colleague or client. Assuming that for legal, ethical, and/or common-sense reasons you decide you must tell a client or colleague something he or she does not want to hear, look for ways to soften the news. For example, suggest options: "No, you cannot do X, but you can accomplish much of your objective by doing Y, which is lawful." Or invite further fact exploration: "Given the currently known facts, you should not do X. However, there might be some additional relevant facts. Is it the case that . . .?"

4. Remain objective. Office memoranda and client advice letters are intended to be predictive: How *will* the law likely resolve a particular problem, not how *should* the law resolve the problem.[3] (The should question is for persuasive writing pieces like briefs.)

What this means is that you should identify both favorable and unfavorable facts, and favorable and unfavorable law, in your memorandum or letter. Do not ignore facts, law, and policies that cut against your proposed solution because they are somehow unfavorable. Do explain the implications to the client if a court were to adopt a view of the law that is contrary to yours. This situation could arise, for example, when you are analyzing an issue of first impression. Having identified the relevant factual and legal universe objectively, you are then free to present your judgment and recommendations.

5. Consider your audience. In a memorandum, you may not need to define legal terms of art and legal phrases because the reader is legally trained. In a client advice letter, you will often need to provide an explanation, rather than rely on the term itself. For example, another lawyer would immediately understand the term "consideration," although you may still have to provide a definition of the term as it applies to your analysis. Conversely, the term "consideration" coupled with a definition probably will not suffice for a non-legally trained audience. Instead, you will have to explain the doctrine and how it relates to your client's problem. You want to be thorough, but you do not want to sound condescending or superior.

---

[3] For a good discussion about the difference, see Mary Dunnewold, *A Tale of Two Issues: "Applying Law to Facts" Versus "Deciding What the Rule Should Be*," 11 Persp. 12 (2002).

What is less obvious is how to treat legal authority, especially in a client advice letter. Citations, as you now know, communicate a great deal about the level and value of the authority used. Consequently, a legally trained reader would consider an analysis without proper citations to authority to be incomplete and potentially incompetent. But a non-lawyer often would not be able to "de-code" the citations. Thus, a question arises as to whether citations should be used in client advice letters. Our advice is to use citations if the reader is legally trained or accustomed to working with lawyers or legal documents.

But even in these situations, use citations sparingly in client advice letters; do not let the citations take the place of providing the necessary detailed analysis the client needs to make an informed decision. If the client has no legal training, then it may not be necessary to provide citations.[4]

A related question is the placement of the citations. Indeed, there is a debate about placement of citations in general.[5] Do they belong within the body of the analysis, or in footnotes? In our view, citations should be placed within the body of a legal memorandum or brief because they are part and parcel of the analysis. While this is also true of the analysis in a client advice letter, we think that placement of citations is more of a personal choice in this situation. We tend to use footnotes in client letters so as to conform to typical letter-writing conventions.

Presentation is also important. Make your written communications reader-friendly. Certainly this includes correct grammar and punctuation. But it also means avoiding overly dense documents. Make liberal use of white space, provide headings and mini-headings, and use lists and charts where appropriate. *Help your readers see your analysis.*

---

[4] Some legal writers use citations in letters to non-legally trained clients because it is always possible that another lawyer will review the letter. For example, the client may seek a second opinion and show the letter to another attorney.

[5] For an overview of the debate, see Bradley G. Clary, *To Note or Not to Note*, 10 Persp. 84 (2002).

6. If your problem will be resolved through application of enacted law, then begin the analysis with that. Recall that legal rules generally find their genesis in enacted law or common law cases. If the rule governing your problem comes from enacted law, start with that language. If the language is clear, you will apply that language. If, as is often the case, the language is ambiguous, then you will try to ascertain the intent of the legislature from the purpose of the enacted law, the type of rule it is, canons of statutory interpretation, the legislative history, court opinions, and, if applicable, agency interpretations[6] A common mistake among beginning legal writers is to start the presentation of any legal analysis by explaining relevant court decisions. This is a natural result of reading first-year law school texts that are primarily casebooks. Begin an enacted law discussion with the enacted law itself. Your presentation of case analysis comes later down the line.

7. If your problem will be resolved through application of case decisions, then undertake a compare and contrast analysis. Recall that the common law develops one case at a time. A court hears a dispute between two or more parties, decides on a rule to apply and a fair result, and issues a decision. Then a court hears a different dispute between two or more parties, decides whether this latest dispute is similar enough to the first one to apply the same rule (and, if not, decides on a different rule to apply), decides on a fair result, and issues a decision. Over many years, the collection of decisions gives rise to a body of legal principles. The lawyer's job in writing a predictive analysis of a client's problem is to compare the current circumstances with those from prior cases, to see how the law might apply.

There is a similar evolution in courts' applications of certain statutory provisions. For example, if the statute requires a buyer to establish that "a seller at the time of contracting had reason to know" of the consequential damages that the buyer is now seeking as a result of the seller's breach, and the statute does not define what constitutes "reason to know," then the problem solver will have to present courts' applications of that statutory provision or element.

How should you present that analysis of cases? There are four basic presentation levels. The fourth level is the most informative and sophisticated.

---

[6] *See e.g.* Bradley G. Clary, *Primer on the Analysis and Presentation of Legal Argument* 32-41 (West 1992); Clary et al., *supra* ch. 1 n. 1, at 21-26.

Level 1: The level one presenter finds a rule in a case, states the rule, cites the case for the rule, and then immediately applies the rule to the facts of the presenter's current problem. The emphasis is on the "black letter" law. The presentation is quick and concise, but involves no analysis of the rule. Thus, a whole piece of the IRAC template is effectively missing, and the presentation is not fully satisfactory.

Example:

In case 1, the court held that the rule governing [insert subject] is [quote rule].

When this rule is applied to our case, it appears that [insert conclusion].

Level 2: The level two presenter finds a rule in a case, states the rule, cites the case for the rule, discusses some facts and logic out of the case, and then applies the rule to the facts of the presenter's current problem. The emphasis is still on the "black letter" law, although the writer engages in some explanation of the rule by referring to the facts and logic in the opinion in the cited case. A level two presentation is more satisfactory than a level one presentation, but again is not fully satisfactory except in circumstances where there is one clear, controlling case that is absolutely "on all fours" with your current problem.[7]

Example:

In case 1, the court held that the rule governing [insert subject] is [quote rule].

The court explained that [insert some of court's logic].

When this rule is applied to our case, it appears that [insert conclusion].

Level 3: The level three presenter formulates a rule from multiple cases, states the rule, marches through the facts and logic of each case one-by-

---

[7] "On all fours" is the classic legal phrase meaning "squarely on point with regard to both facts and law . . . ." Bryan A. Garner, *A Dictionary of Modern Legal Usage* 618 (2d ed., Oxford U. Press 1995).

one (citing each case as he goes), and then applies the rule at the end of the sequence to the facts of the presenter's current problem. This is a more sophisticated approach than the previous two. It does embody complete Rule and Analysis/Application segments of the IRAC template. And it may be a useful approach in helping a reader to understand the development of a particular rule of law. It can result in a competent treatment of a problem. However, it does not involve a *synthesis* of patterns. It is a forced march through cases individually. Thus, it leaves to a reader much of the work of comparing the cases to see how the similarities and dissimilarities match up.

Example:

In cases 1, 2, and 3, the courts held that the rule governing [insert subject] is [quote rule].

The court in case 1 explained that [insert some of court's logic].

The court in case 2 explained that [insert some of court's logic].

The court in case 3 explained that [insert some of court's logic].

When this rule is applied to our case, it appears that [insert conclusion].

Level 4: The level four presenter formulates a rule from multiple cases, states the rule, *synthesizes the patterns* from the cases, identifies the facts and logic common to the patterns, and then applies the rule consistently with the most appropriate pattern to the presenter's current problem.

Example:

The rule relevant to this case is X. Its elements are a, b, and c. Element c is contested in our case. Element c was at issue in six major cases in our jurisdiction.

In cases 1, 2, and 3, element c was found to be satisfied, and the plaintiff recovered for his injury because . . . [synthesize pattern].

In cases 4, 5, and 6, element c was found not to be satisfied, and the plaintiff did not recover for his injury because . . . [synthesize pattern].

The pattern in the present case is more like the pattern found in cases 1, 2, and 3 because . . . [explain].

Therefore, a court analyzing our facts likely will find that element c is satisfied, and our client should recover for her injury.

Alternatively, the level four presenter may find it helpful to bifurcate the analysis. In this model of presentation, she would first synthesize the pattern in those cases to which she is analogizing. She would immediately apply the reasoning of those cases, demonstrating why a similar result is justified. Then she would synthesize the pattern in those cases she is distinguishing and apply the reasoning of those cases, demonstrating that a different result is justified.

Example:

The rule relevant to this case is X. Its elements are a, b, and c. Element c is contested in our case. Element c was at issue in six major cases in our jurisdiction.

In cases 1, 2, and 3, element c was found to be satisfied, and the plaintiff recovered for his injury because . . . [synthesize pattern].

The facts in the instant case are like the pattern found in cases 1, 2, and 3 because . . . [explain].

Conversely, in cases 4, 5, and 6, element c was found not to be satisfied, and the plaintiff did not recover for his injury because . . . [synthesize pattern].

These cases are distinguishable. In the instant case [explain why and how the cases are distinguishable].

Therefore, a court analyzing our facts likely will find that element c is satisfied, and our client likely will should for her injury.

We encourage you to adopt the level four approach, or a combination of the level three and four approaches, as often as you can, when presenting an analysis to your reader.

THE OFFICE MEMORANDUM TEMPLATE

Putting together everything you know so far, how might you prepare a standard office memorandum? The following is a template you might use, employing a version of an IRAC structure to discuss the tortious interference with contract cases described in the "Assembling a rule from multiple court decisions" section from Chapter 5, at pages 50-53. The citations in this template conform to the *ALWD Citation Manual*.

For purposes of the sample memorandum, assume that the lawyer writing it has been presented with the following problem:

> The lawyer's best client is Acme Company, a civil engineering firm. For some time, Acme has had a written contract to obtain customized computer software from ABC Corporation. Acme and ABC each have the right to terminate the contract at will, upon giving 30 days advance notice to the other party. ABC designs and makes the software from proprietary specifications provided by Acme under a confidentiality agreement that survives any termination of the contract. Acme's specifications are considered an Acme trade secret, and are zealously guarded.

> Raider Company is in the same engineering business as Acme, but is not a direct competitor in the sense that, although it serves a lot of the same customers, it offers different services to them than Acme does. Raider has approached ABC to purchase customized software. Raider is aware of Acme's contract with ABC. Acme's business people have reason to believe that Raider has offered ABC incentives to enter into a lucrative software supply agreement, provided that ABC terminates its existing software supply deal with Acme, and also provided that ABC allows Raider to see Acme's

confidential software specifications before ABC surrenders those back to Acme as part of the termination process.

Acme has now come to the lawyer and asked the following question: If ABC terminates its software supply agreement with Acme, and the incentives prove to be true, does Acme have any recourse against Raider?

Assume for purposes of the sample memorandum template that the only relevant cases are the *RJM Sales & Marketing, Hough Transit, Oak Park Development*, and *J.N.R. Enterprises* decisions discussed in Chapter 5 of this text. The lawyer's office memorandum to a senior partner, along with our editorial annotations in the right-hand margin, follows.

MEMORANDUM	Title in all caps, and either in bold or underlined.
To: Senior Partner	Basic information: To, From, Date, and Subject. "Re:" section typically includes the parties, the issue, and the relevant law.
From: Young Associate	
Date: Oct. XX, 20XX	
Re: Tortious Interference with a Terminable-at-Will Contract between Acme and ABC.	
Question Presented	Heading
Can Acme Company ("Acme") sue Raider Company ("Raider") under the doctrine of tortious interference with contract if Raider procures termination of Acme's existing software contract with ABC Corporation ("ABC") and, in the process, obtains access to Acme's propriety software specifications without Acme's consent?	The client's "big picture" question, framed in specific terms, using relevant names and key facts.
Short Answer	Heading
Yes, there is a cause of action against Raider for tortious interference with the Acme-ABC contract under those circumstances because Raider will have committed an independent tort in connection with the termination of the contract.	Give the reader an answer to the question presented. Try to start with yes or no, and then add a "because."
Facts	Heading
For some time, Acme has had a written contract to obtain customized computer software from ABC Corporation. Acme and ABC each has the right to terminate the contract at will upon giving 30 days advance notice to the other party. ABC designs the software from proprietary specifications provided by Acme under a confidentiality	Tell the relevant fact story. Be concise, especially if you are writing the memo to an internal audience who is already

agreement that survives any termination of the contract. Acme's specifications are considered an Acme trade secret and are zealously guarded.

Raider Company is in the same engineering business as Acme, but Raider is not a direct competitor in the sense that, although it serves many of the same customers, it offers different services to them than Acme does. Raider has approached ABC to purchase customized software. Raider is aware of Acme's contract with ABC. Acme's business people have reason to believe that Raider has offered ABC incentives to enter into a lucrative software supply agreement, provided that (1) ABC terminates its existing software supply deal with Acme, and (2) ABC allows Raider to see Acme's confidential software specifications before ABC surrenders those back to Acme as part of the termination process.

Analysis

The Doctrine Of Tortious Interference With A Terminable-At-Will Contract Requires A Wrongful Act That Procures A Breach Of The Relevant Contract Or That Is Accompanied By Other Independently Wrongful, Actionable Conduct.

A cause of action for tortious interference with a contract requires "(1) the existence of a contract, (2) the alleged tortfeasor's knowledge of that contract, (3) the intentional interference with the contract, (4) without justification, and (5) damages resulting from the interference." *Oak Park Dev. Co. v. Snyder Bro. of Minn., Inc.*, 499 N.W.2d 500, 505 (Minn. App. 1993).

In the present circumstance, two of these elements are uncontested. There is a contract between Acme and ABC. Raider is aware of that contract. The balance of this Memorandum will focus only on the remaining three

---

*Side notes:*

generally familiar with the facts. But do not neglect to identify the key facts—they drive the legal analysis. Further, if someone is reviewing your memo at some future time, the fact section will be critical to understanding why you gave the legal advice you did.

Heading

Mini-heading, framed in generic terms, to introduce the analysis.

Provide the rule, with an appropriate citation to authority. (Note that in this example, the rule is already conveniently framed in its constituent elements.)

Expressly identify undisputed elements, and take

elements.

them as given.

A. Is Raider Intentionally Interfering With The Acme-ABC Contract?

Provide a subheading for each contested element, framed as a question, introducing the disputed element.

Intentional interference means that a defendant has "induced [another] party to breach [the relevant] contract or that the defendant intentionally interfered with the plaintiff's contractual rights by committing an independent tort." *J.N.R. Enter., Inc. v. Frigidaire Co.*, No. C5-98-2281, 1999 WL 377747, at *3 (Minn. App. June 1, 1999) (unpublished).

Provide a statement of the element. (Note that we cite to an unpublished opinion. Recall that in Minnesota, unpublished opinions may be cited and subsequent courts may adopt the reasoning.)

Historically, Minnesota courts did not recognize a claim for tortious interference with a terminable-at-will contract. *Hough Transit, Ltd. v. Natl. Farmers Org.*, 472 N.W.2d 358, 361 (Minn. App. 1991); *RJM Sales & Mktg., Inc. v. Banfi Prod. Corp.*, 546 F. Supp. 1368, 1378 (D. Minn. 1982). Recently, however, the Minnesota Court of Appeals has abandoned that view. *J.N.R. Enter.*, 1999 WL 377747, at *3; *Oak Park Dev.*, 499 N.W.2d at 505.

But "intentionally interfering" with a terminable-at-will contract requires that the company commit an independent tort that actually interferes with the contract. This is because interference with a terminable-at-will contract does not necessarily rise to the level of tortious conduct when either party was free lawfully to terminate the contract upon giving proper notice. Consequently, to maintain a suit against Raider for tortious interference with the present terminable-at-will contract, Acme will have to establish that Raider committed an independently wrongful act in connection with the termination of the contract.

Develop the rule section by explaining what the element means.

There is only one case among the four applicable to Acme's situation where the court permitted a plaintiff to continue with a claim that a defendant had tortiously interfered with a terminable-at-will contract between the plaintiff and another party. In *J.N.R. Enterprises*, 1999 WL

Begin to synthesize the pattern in the cases, looking at both the court's language and the results. (Where,

377747, at *4, the court allowed the plaintiff to proceed with a tortious interference action because the defendant had allegedly defamed the plaintiff. Although this is an unpublished opinion, it represents the court's clearest statement of the emerging rule with respect to intentional interference with terminable-at-will contracts. This case is particularly relevant because Acme's situation is similar to J.N.R. Enterprises' in that Raider is seeking access to Acme's proprietary design information—which may be a tortious act—in connection with urging ABC to terminate the Acme-ABC contract.

By contrast, the courts have refused to permit a plaintiff to proceed when there was no independently tortious conduct. In *Oak Park Development*, the court refused to allow the plaintiff to proceed with a tortious interference action when the plaintiff's only proof was that the defendant offered a superior deal to the third party. 499 N.W.2d at 506. In *Hough Transit*, the court refused to allow the plaintiff to proceed and noted that even if Minnesota permitted a claim for tortious interference with a terminable-at-will contract (which it did not at that time), the plaintiff could not show that any of the defendant's actions were independently wrongful. 472 N.W.2d at 361. Finally, in *RJM Sales & Marketing*, the court refused to allow the plaintiff to proceed and stated that jurisdictions recognizing a claim for tortious interference with a terminable-at-will contract require a plaintiff to prove " 'concomitant un-conscionable conduct' . . . such as misappropriation of trade secrets. . . ." 546 F. Supp. at 1378 (internal citation omitted).

Thus, the pattern that emerges in these cases is that a plaintiff must be able to establish that a defendant committed an independently wrongful act in connection with urging a party to breach the relevant terminable-at-will contract.

These cases are distinguishable and actually reinforce Acme's position. If Raider is successful in getting ABC to

---

Margin notes:

as here, you have a spectrum of authority, you may want to apply the rule and reasoning of the cases to which you are analogizing. Or, you may want to discuss all of the cases before applying them. See the margin note on the next page.)

Do not avoid unfavorable authority. Provide it, address it, and then attempt to do something with it.

Complete synthesizing the pattern in the cases.

Apply the law to the instant facts and conclude. (In

terminate its contract with Acme and, in connection with the termination, ABC gives Raider access to Acme's proprietary design information, then Raider has committed an independently wrongful action. Acme's proprietary design information constitutes a trade secret. Under these circumstances, Acme would be able to satisfy this element.

Acme's position is consistent with the policy behind "tortious interference" law. In the commercial arena, all kinds of activities may "interfere" with contracts. If all of those interferences were "tortious," the courts would be deluged with lawsuits, and businesses (including Acme) would be reluctant to act. Yet, at the same time, commercial activity must be reasonable and fair. Concluding that Raider's conduct is actionable is consistent with the balance struck by the current rule.

B. Does Raider Have A Justification For Its Conduct?

The court in *J.N.R. Enterprises* noted that there is a "competitor's privilege" that might justify a defendant's interference with a terminable-at-will contract. 1999 WL 377747, at *4. The court commented that a promise by a defendant to another party to double its business is simply good competition. *See id.*

Acme has two strong arguments if Raider were to claim a competitor's privilege. First, Raider is not truly a competitor. Raider offers different services than does Acme. Thus, Raider should not be able to rely on a competition privilege.

Second, and alternatively, even if Raider is a competitor, Raider is employing wrongful means to compete with Acme. It is unlawful to misappropriate trade secrets, as the *RJM Sales & Marketing* court made clear. Thus, Raider's actions are not protected by the competitor's privilege.

Sidebar annotations:

this part of the application, the cases are distinguished. In other words, the rule and application sections are bifurcated. It would also be permissible to synthesize the pattern from all of the cases, identify the facts and reasoning common to the cases, and then apply them to the instant facts.) Further, think about whether your conclusion is consistent with the policies behind the legal rule.

Repeat the steps for the next element. Introduce it and provide the rule.

Apply the rule.

Conclude.

C. Will Acme Suffer Damages From Raider's Conduct?

This part of the equation is less clear on the facts known to date. Acme will suffer injury from Raider's unauthorized access to Acme proprietary design specifications. Exactly how much injury is another question.

I recommend we ask for calculations as to the value of the specifications, any additional cost to Acme from having to procure production of the software from another company, and similar information.

Conclusion

In summary, Acme likely has a viable cause of action against Raider if Raider procures a termination of the ABC agreement with Acme and, in the process, obtains unauthorized access to Acme proprietary design information in exchange for offering a lucrative deal to ABC. All of the elements of tortious interference are present. First, there is a contract between ABC-Acme. Second, Raider knows about that agreement. Third, Raider is using improper methods to procure a termination of the agreement, even if the termination is technically not a breach of the agreement because it is terminable at will on thirty days notice. Fourth, Raider may not rely on a competitor's privilege as justification for its actions, because Raider is not a direct competitor and in any event must not engage in misappropriation of trade secrets when it tries to claim a competition privilege. Fifth, damages likely will result, although calculations should be completed to verify what those are.

Repeat the steps as to the next element.

Note that there may be times when you would like more facts with which to perform a sound analysis. Do not be afraid to talk with your client or colleagues about those, and see if you can get them.

Formally conclude.

THE CLIENT ADVICE LETTER
TEMPLATE

How would you prepare a standard client letter, using the same problem and authority presented in the sample office memorandum? The following template also employs the IRAC structure, demonstrating one way to organize the letter. Again, we want to emphasize that this is not the only way to present the analysis. If your legal writing professor prefers another structure, then you should adapt the following sample to conform to his or her template.

In the sample client advice letter below, the client is once again Acme and the letter is addressed to the Vice President for Risk Management, who routinely works with attorneys. As with the Office Memorandum Template, the citations generally conform to the *ALWD Citation Manual*.

Cray & Haslyt, P. C.

Attorneys and Counselors at Law
333 Not Real Street
No Place, Minnesota 1234X
555.555.5555

October XX, 20XX

Mr. Jonathon Drake
Vice President of Risk Management
Acme Company
111 Any Street
Any Town, Minnesota 1255X

Re: Contract Interference by Raider Company

Dear Mr. Drake:

We have had an opportunity to review whether Acme has any recourse against Raider Company if Raider successfully causes ABC Corporation to terminate its contract with Acme and, in the process, Raider improperly obtains access to Acme's proprietary software specifications. In brief, we conclude that under these circumstances, Acme would have a cause of action against Raider because Raider's intentional conduct is accompanied by Raider's theft of a trade secret.

Our conclusion, while not a guaranty of how a court would ultimately rule, is based on relevant cases from the Minnesota courts as applied to the facts you presented to us, as well as the Acme-ABC contract we reviewed.

Facts

Acme has a written contract with ABC to obtain customized computer software. Each party has the right to terminate the contract at will upon giving 30 days advance

Letterhead of firm	
Date	
Address of recipient	
Reference	
Provide opening paragraphs that connect with the client; state the issue in terms the client can understand; provide a brief answer to the client's question. Explain that your conclusion is not a guaranty of how a court will rule, but that it is a prediction of how a court would likely rule in light of the current law as applied to the facts.	
State the facts, as provided from the client and any other source from which you	

notice to the other party. ABC designs the software from proprietary specifications that Acme provides to ABC under a confidentiality agreement that survives any termination of the contract. Acme's specifications are considered an Acme trade secret and are zealously guarded.	obtained the facts.
Raider is in the same business as Acme. They are not, however, direct competitors because, although they serve many of the same customers, Raider offers different services to these clients than does Acme. Raider is aware of Acme's contract with ABC.	
Acme executives have learned that Raider recently approached ABC to purchase customized software. Moreover, Acme executives have reason to believe that Raider has offered incentives to ABC to enter into a lucrative software supply agreement with Raider, provided that (1) ABC terminates its existing software supply deal with Acme, and (2) ABC allows Raider to see Acme's confidential software specifications before ABC surrenders them to Acme as part of the ABC/Acme contract termination.	
If these facts have changed since we met last week, or if there are additional facts not known to us, please contact the law firm because our analysis could change.	Suggest that if the facts are not as stated here, then the analysis could change.
### Explanation	
Acme's recourse against Raider would be to file suit for tortious interference with a contract. To prevail, Acme will have to establish the following five elements: (1) there is a contract between Acme and ABC; (2) Raider has knowledge of that contract; (3) Raider has intentionally interfered with that contract; (4) Raider has no justification to interfere with that contract; and (5) Acme has incurred	Provide an introduction, which includes a conclusion and an implicit organizational structure—the elements of the claim that comprise the rule.

damages as a result of Raider's intentional interference.[1]

In Acme's situation, elements 1 and 2 are uncontested: There is a contract between Acme and ABC, and Raider is aware of that contract. The last three elements, however, need further examination and explanation.

> Focus on those elements that need further explanation. Introduce the elements.

1. Is Raider Intentionally Interfering With The Acme-ABC Contract?

In general, "intentional interference with a contractual relationship" means that a company (such as Raider) induced a party (such as ABC) to breach the relevant contract (such as the Acme-ABC contract) or that the company intentionally interfered with the parties' contractual rights by committing an independent, wrongful act.[2]

> Provide the rule.

Historically, there was no recourse against a company like Raider when the contract interfered with was "terminable at will," which is the type of contract between Acme and ABC.[3] The Minnesota Court of Appeals, however, now recognizes tortious interference with a terminable-at-will contract.[4] But "intentionally interfering" with a terminable-at-will contract requires that the company

> Provide an explanation of the rule, which includes a discussion of the cases.

---

[1] The Minnesota Court of Appeals set forth the elements of a tortious interference with a contract claim in *Oak Park Dev. Co. v. Snyder Bro. of Minn., Inc.*, 499 N.W.2d 500, 505 (Minn. App. 1993).

[2] *J.N.R. Enter., Inc. v. Frigidaire Co.*, No. C5-98-2281, 1999 WL 377747 at *3 (Minn. App. June 1, 1999) (unpublished).

[3] *See Hough Transit, Ltd. Natl. Farmers Org.*, 472 N.W.2d 356, 361 (Minn. App. 1991); *RJM Sales & Mktg., Inc. v. Banfi Prod. Corp.*, 546 F. Supp. 1368, 1378 (D. Minn. 1982).

[4] *See Oak Park Dev.*, 499 N.W.2d at 506; *J.N.R. Enter.*, 1999 WL 377747 at *3.

commit an independent wrong that actually interferes with the contract. This is because interference with a terminable-at-will contract does not necessarily rise to the level of wrongful conduct—tortious conduct—when either party was free lawfully to terminate the contract upon giving proper notice. Consequently, to maintain a suit against Raider for tortious interference with the present terminable-at-will contract, Acme will have to establish that Raider committed an independently wrongful act in connection with the termination of the contract.

There is only one case among the four applicable to Acme's situation where the court permitted a plaintiff to continue with a claim that a defendant had tortiously interfered with a terminable-at-will contract between the plaintiff and another party. In *J.N.R. Enterprises v. Frigidaire Co.*, the court allowed the plaintiff to proceed with a tortious interference action because the defendant had allegedly defamed the plaintiff. This is an "unpublished opinion," which means that while it is not authoritative, it can be cited as an authority and the court's reasoning may be adopted by later courts. Acme's situation is similar to J.N.R. Enterprises' in that Raider is seeking access to Acme's proprietary design information, which may be an independently wrongful act—a tortious act—in connection with urging ABC to terminate the Acme-ABC contract.

By contrast, the courts have refused to permit a plaintiff to proceed when there was no independently tortious conduct. In *Oak Park Development*, the court refused to allow the plaintiff to proceed with a tortious interference action when the plaintiff's only proof was that the defendant offered a superior deal to the third party. In *Hough Transit*, the court refused to allow the plaintiff to proceed and noted that even if Minnesota permitted a claim for tortious interference with a terminable-at-will contract (which it did not at that time), the plaintiff could not show that any of the defendant's actions were independently

---

Margin notes:

Begin to synthesize the pattern in the cases. (Where, as here, you have a spectrum of authority, you may want to apply the rule and reasoning of the cases to which you are comparing. Or you may want to discuss all of the cases before applying them. See the margin note on the next page.)

Complete synthesizing the cases.

wrongful. Finally, in *RJM Sales & Marketing*, the court refused to allow the plaintiff to proceed and stated that jurisdictions recognizing a claim for tortious interference with a terminable-at-will contract require a plaintiff to prove " 'concomitant, unconscionable conduct' . . . such as misappropriation of trade secrets. . . ."[5] Thus, the pattern that emerges in these cases is that a plaintiff must be able to establish that a defendant committed an independently wrongful act in connection with urging a party to breach the relevant terminable-at-will contract.

These cases are distinguishable and actually reinforce Acme's position. If Raider is successful in getting ABC to terminate its contract with Acme and, in connection with the termination, ABC gives Raider access to Acme's proprietary design information, then Raider has committed an independently wrongful action. Acme's proprietary design information constitutes a trade secret. Under these circumstances, Acme would be able to satisfy this element.

This conclusion is consistent with the general public policy that appears to be evolving, as evidenced in the most recent, albeit unpublished, opinion by the Minnesota Court of Appeals that balances freedom of action and fair dealing.

2. Does Raider Have A Justification For Its Conduct?

Raider could claim that it has a "competitor's privilege," which justifies its interference with Acme's terminable-at-will contract with ABC. In the *J.N.R. Enterprises* case, the court noted that a defendant's interference with a terminable-at-will contract may be justified by a "competitor's privilege." More specifically, the court commented that a promise by a defendant to a

Apply to the facts. (In this sample, the cases are distinguished. It would also be permissible to synthesize the pattern from all the cases on this element, identify the facts and reasoning common to the cases, and then apply them.)

Conclude.

Repeat for the next element. Provide an introduction.

Provide the rule.

---

[5] 546 F. Supp. at 1378 (internal citation omitted).

third party to double its business is simply good competition. But the court also stated that a defendant may not employ wrongful means.

Acme has two strong arguments if Raider were to claim a competitor's privilege. First, Raider is not truly a competitor. Raider offers different services than does Acme. Thus, Raider should not be able to rely on a competition privilege.

Apply the rule.

Second, and alternatively, even if Raider is a competitor, Raider is employing wrongful means to compete with Acme. It is unlawful to misappropriate trade secrets, as the *RJM Sales & Marketing* court made clear. Thus, Raider's actions are not protected by the competitor's privilege.

Conclude.

3. Will Acme Suffer Damages From Raider's Conduct?

Repeat for the next element. Introduce the issue. Provide the rule; apply the rule; conclude.

To prevail, Acme must establish that it suffered damages. Although it appears that Acme will suffer injury from Raider's unauthorized access to Acme's proprietary design specifications, it's not clear precisely how, and how much Acme will be damaged.

Therefore, we recommend calculating the value of the specifications, any additional cost to Acme from having to procure production of the software from another company, and any other relevant information.

Summary

If Raider is able to procure a termination of the Acme-ABC contract and, in the process, obtains unauthorized access to Acme proprietary design information in exchange for offering a lucrative deal to ABC, then Acme will be able to bring suit against Raider. Acme will

Formally conclude and provide a summary. If specific recommendations are necessary, include them here.

be able to establish all of the elements of a tortious-interference-with-contract claim. First, there is an Acme-ABC contract. Second, Raider knows of that contract. Third, Raider will have committed an independent, wrongful act to procure ABC's termination of the agreement. Fourth, Raider may not rely on a competitor's privilege as justification for its actions. Fifth, damages will likely result, although precise calculations should be completed to determine the amount of those damages.

Please do not hesitate to contact us if you have any questions. We would be happy to meet with you.

Very truly yours,

Benson Cray

Benson Cray

Reconnect with your client.

Closing

CHAPTER 12

Communicating a Persuasive Analysis

In the previous chapter, we provided fundamental templates for two forms of predictive writing, office memoranda and client letters. Now, in this final chapter, we provide fundamental templates for two forms of persuasive writing, trial court and appellate court briefs.[1] First, however, we will provide basic principles that apply to both forms of persuasive writing.

---

[1] As was true of the predictive writing examples, our examples of trial court and appellate court briefs are not intended to provide the only way to present a persuasive analysis. If your particular audience prefers or requires a different format, use that one. In the case of court briefs, each jurisdiction has rules concerning the technical aspects of format. These rules govern such topics as the sequence of the components, margin sizes, font types and sizes, paper size, length, use of numbered or non-numbered paper, use of covers, colors of covers, and the like. Ignore these rules at your peril. Failure to follow them can result in rejection of your briefs.

Because the technical rules vary from court to court, we do not claim that our models comply with the requirements in every court. We do intend, however, to provide models that illustrate the basic concepts inherent in good persuasive writing and that illustrate the format that is relatively standard in many trial and appellate courts.

COMMON FEATURES OF GOOD PERSUASIVE WRITING

1. In either a trial court brief or an appellate court brief, use some version of the IRAC template. All court briefs do the following: identify the problem to be addressed, present the legal rule that will govern the problem, analyze the rule, apply the rule to the specific facts of the problem, and formulate a conclusion that tells the court how the law should resolve the problem. Notice how this is different from the use of the IRAC template in the predictive setting. Now you are arguing how the law *should* apply, not just exploring how it *will* apply.

2. Offer a solution to a problem. You are still in the problem-solving business. Your clients and colleagues do not want mere interesting discussions, nor does the court to which you are directing the brief. The court wants to know your client's view as to the proper legal resolution of the dispute that is already in litigation. So assert that view. Do so positively and with conviction.

3. Offer a solution that is favorable to your client. Your job in a brief is to present your client's view of the case as favorably as you can. So try to do that. If the best you can do is, "the other side wins," then you should have settled the matter.

Recognize, however, that in presenting your case, you may not mislead the court. You have a duty to zealously advocate for your client, but you are simultaneously an officer of the court.[2] Do not dwell on bad facts, but do not pretend they are not there. Face them and move on. Similarly, do not ignore bad legal precedent. Face it and move on.

How do you face bad facts and legal authorities? There are four classic approaches:

---

[2] "A lawyer is a representative of clients, an officer of the legal system, and a public citizen having special responsibility for the quality of justice." Preamble to the Minnesota Rules of Professional Conduct (2002). This is a standard concept, applicable as well in other jurisdictions.

➤ Claim that the facts and/or the authorities are not actually bad by using them affirmatively in support of your position. It is not unusual for facts and authorities to be double-edged, good for one party from one standpoint, but good for the other party from another standpoint. ("What this fact really proves is . . . ." "What this case really stands for is . . . .")

➤ Claim that the facts and/or the authorities do not matter. Not every bad fact or authority will be relevant to the case because the case will be resolved on another basis. ("The court may disregard this fact because it is not material to the application of the relevant threshold rule." "The court may disregard this case because it does not reflect the law in this jurisdiction on the point at issue.")

➤ Claim that the facts and/or the authorities are distinguishable. ("This fact is only unfavorable when combined with certain other facts that are not present in the instant case." "This case only reached [an unfavorable result] because the court based its decision on a combination of factors that are not all present in the instant case.")

➤ Claim that the facts and/or the authorities are simply wrong. ("This case assumed the existence of [fact x], and [fact x] is simply not true." "The court adopted the view of only two other courts, while ten courts have rejected that view as incorrect.")

4. Advocate. Your job now is to convince a court "that society's interest in drawing a line in a particular place, in order to resolve a case or controversy, coincides with the client's interest in winning particular relief."[3] Ask yourself the following questions:

➤ What relief *does* my client want?

➤ What argument will convince a court that the relief my client wants is also in the best interest of a broader constituency—the public, the court system, specific third parties, etc.?

---

[3] Clary, *supra* ch. 11 n. 6, at 7.

➢ In what sequence do I have to make my points so that they lead to the desired conclusion?

5. Focus on the factual story to tell. Recall that facts drive legal results. How you tell the story of the case will matter significantly. As you present the facts, try to follow these tips:

➢ Make sure there is a logical beginning, middle, and end to your fact recitation.

➢ Make sure you cover all the material facts that drive the legal result.

➢ Try to start strong and end strong.

➢ To the extent you can, make the characters come alive. Give the court a sense of the kind of people with whom it is dealing on one or both sides of the case, if that is to your advantage. (Of course, sometimes it is not to your advantage.) Additionally, once you have identified the parties' legal designations, use their names or a suitably descriptive noun in your argument.

➢ Think about what in the story makes it interesting. Even the most technical of legal issues arises from a clash among people and ideas. Draw the court's attention to that clash.[4]

6. If your problem will be resolved through application of enacted law, begin your analysis with that. Recall that legal rules generally find their genesis in enacted law or common law cases. If the rule governing your problem comes from enacted law, start with that language. If the language is clear, you will apply that language. If, as is often the case, the language is

---

[4] There is an art to story-telling that goes well beyond the scope of this text. If you wish to learn more about that art, you might read such literature as Tom Galbraith, *Storytelling: The Anecdotal Antidote*, 28 Litig. 17-23 (2002). Galbraith reminds us that "[s]uccess in litigation revolves around two questions: What is legally important, and what is emotionally persuasive? The difference is that of the head and the heart. Law school and, increasingly, apprenticeship instruct the head and ignore the heart. As an antidote, I offer this suggestion: Come back to the oldest art form. Storytelling will teach you how to move an audience." *Id.* at 23.

ambiguous, then you will try to ascertain the intent of the legislature from the purpose of the enacted law, the type of rule it is, standard canons of interpretation, the legislative history, court opinions, and, if applicable, agency interpretations.[5] But begin an enacted law discussion with the enacted law itself.

7. If your problem will be resolved through application of case decisions, then undertake a compare-and-contrast analysis. Recall that the common law develops one problem at a time. As we have said before, a court hears a dispute between two or more parties, decides on a rule to apply, determines the result, and issues a decision. Then a court hears a different dispute between two or more parties, decides whether this latest dispute is similar enough to the first one to apply the same rule (and, if not, decides on a different rule to apply), determines the result, and issues a decision. Over many years, the collection of decisions gives rise to a body of legal principles. The lawyer's job in writing a persuasive analysis of a client's problem for a court is to compare the current circumstances with those from prior cases, to argue how the law *should* apply.

8. Start with your "high ground." Consistent with other fundamental principles, try where possible to start on your high ground and stay there as long as you can. Lead with strength. You may, of course, adopt an "even if" structure. For example, "My client wins for [reason number 1], but EVEN IF the Court adopts a different view, my client still wins for [reason number 2]."

Note two things about "even if" arguments. First, using too many of them will dilute the strength of your best position. Second, sometimes "even if" arguments work better with legal points than factual ones. It is hard, for example, to argue "My client was not at the scene. But even if he was, my client did not shoot the gun." On the other hand, it is not too implausible to argue "The Court should interpret [legal rule] as meaning [X], but even if the Court interprets the rule to mean [Y], then my client still wins because . . . ."

9. Consider your audience. Notice that you are now writing for a judge or judges (although other relevant audiences will include your client,

---

[5] *See e.g.* Clary, *supra* ch. 11 n. 6, at 32-41; Clary et al., *supra* ch. 1 n. 1, at 21-26.

your colleagues, and your adversaries). What are some of the features of judges as an audience?

> ➢ Judges are legally trained and may already be familiar with your type of legal problem from experience with other disputes. Indeed, judges may be the authors of the very authorities you are discussing. Know what perspective your specific judge (or judges) brings to your case.

> ➢ Judges are busy. They have too much to do, and too little time within which to do it. What does this mean? First, it means be plain. Do not assume that just because a judge is legally trained you can simply skip over parts of the legal analysis. Second, be concise. There is a reason why arguments to the court are called briefs.

> ➢ Judges expect you to give them deference and to treat opposing counsel deferentially. Judges do not like *ad hominem* personal attacks on your adversaries. ("I regret to have to inform the Court that Mr. X is a lying scumbag." *Do not say this.*) Judges expect civility. Let the facts and the law speak for themselves.

> ➢ Judges expect a certain degree of formality, i.e., no use of slang terms or colloquialisms unless those are peculiarly relevant to the specific facts of the dispute.

In addition, as you consider your audience, think about ways to present information that will be helpful. Lists are useful presentation devices in briefs, just as they are in predictive writing. List the elements of relevant legal rules. List helpful facts, and link that list to the legal element to which the facts pertain. Sometimes putting the lists in charts or tables can be visually appealing. *Help the court to see your analysis.*

10.   Pay attention to the standard of review or burden of proof the court will have to apply in reaching a decision. Courts do not always get to decide questions in any manner they may wish. For example, you will learn in your federal civil procedure course that a district court reviewing a Rule 12(b)(6) motion to dismiss a complaint on its face must take the facts pleaded in the complaint as true for purposes of the motion. A federal district court reviewing a Rule 56 summary judgment motion may not decide disputed issues of material fact. An appellate court reviewing a district court decision on a matter of law will typically review that decision *de novo* and substitute the appellate court's own view of that law, but an appellate court ordinarily must defer to a district court's fact findings unless those findings are clearly erroneous. There are a number of important procedural rules relating to the standards that courts must use to review certain kinds of questions at specific stages of proceedings. Your briefs typically should remind the court of the relevant standards of review.

THE TRIAL COURT BRIEF TEMPLATE

Putting together everything you know so far, how might you prepare a standard federal district court brief?

As you review the sample trial court papers that follow at page 183, notice some of the following components.

The Motion Itself

Requests for a ruling from a trial court are normally made by written notice and motion. The notice tells the court and all of the lawyers in the case that the moving party will be requesting a hearing from the judge at a particular day, time, and place. The motion tells the court and lawyers what order the moving party wants, and recites a short-hand version of the grounds. The motion also typically identifies for the court and lawyers the materials upon which the moving party relies to support the motion. Sometimes the notice and the motion are combined into a single document for efficiency.

The Introduction to the Legal Memorandum

The purpose of this section is to provide the court with a brief introduction to the issue or issues. As you will recall, judges are busy people and they want to know up front two things: "What do you want me to do, counsel, and why should I do that?"[6]

---

[6] One of the authors was in court when a United States Magistrate Judge literally began an oral argument on a motion with those very words to the assembled lawyers.

The Introduction sets the focus for the rest of the brief. It tells the court why, based on precedent and policy, your client should win. Developing a focus is an important part of persuasive writing, especially when writing to a court. The focus often acts as the glue that holds together the various arguments. For example, if your client has been charged with conspiracy to commit first-degree murder, and your research reveals that an agreement—express or implied—is an essential element of finding a conspiracy, then one focus you may select is that your client never agreed to the conspiracy. Your brief would emphasize those facts that would lead the trier of fact to conclude that there is no evidence on that point.

Some judges, and some professors, require a question presented or statement of the issue in this section. There are several ways to construct a question presented, which are discussed in the section of this book on appellate briefs because that is the context in which the requirement is most likely to arise.

Statement of Facts

In working with the facts, it is often useful to categorize facts as either material (directly legally significant) or contextual. Material facts are those facts that are critical to resolving the client's problem—the facts that drive the analysis. Contextual facts are not essential to the analysis, but provide important background for "selling" the story. Contextual facts may lend an emotional edge to the story, for example, and experienced advocates know that judicious use of emotional facts can help to make their clients appear sympathetic. Be cautious, though. Inexperienced advocates sometimes rely too heavily on emotional facts, which may cause the reader to recoil.

Sometimes facts will be undisputed. Alternatively, the parties may stipulate that the facts are undisputed for the limited purposes of a specific motion. ("Your Honor, even assuming the facts are exactly as [the adversary] wishes they were, we still win this motion as a matter of law because . . . .") Often, however, the parties will not agree on the facts for any purposes. In any case, it is the advocate's job is to put her client's best foot forward while ensuring as an officer of the court that all material facts—favorable and unfavorable—are accounted for.

Those facts that are favorable should be given greater emphasis. Those that are unfavorable should be given less emphasis. The easiest way to emphasize facts is to place them at the beginning or ending of paragraphs. Similarly, to deemphasize facts, place them in the middle of a paragraph. Many readers look predominantly at the first and last sentences of a paragraph and tend to skim over the middle section. Minimizing unfavorable facts by placing them between favorable facts promotes reader attention to the favorable ones.

Argument Point Headings

Crafting persuasive point headings is an applied art. They take time, patience, and skill. In general, for each issue, there should be a major point heading. This point heading introduces the argument for that issue. Often, however, there is more than one argument for each issue. In those cases, the major point heading is stated in general terms, often in a way that previews your focus. Then the minor point headings introduce each discrete argument.

For example, assume that your client has been charged with violating the federal drug analogue statute. Further assume that you have a legitimate argument that the relevant section under which your client was charged is ambiguous because it is not textually clear whether the definition of an analogue requires a conjunctive reading (subsection i must be satisfied _plus_ either subsection ii or iii) or a disjunctive reading (_only one_ of subsections i, ii, or iii must be satisfied). Finally, assume that you have authority for the proposition that Congress never intended the statute to reach your client's conduct.

Example of Major and Minor Point Headings:

I. The Definition of a Controlled Substance Analogue Must Be Read in the Conjunctive.

A. The term "controlled substance" is ambiguous.
B. The legislative history supports a conjunctive interpretation of the term.
C. Under the rule of lenity, an ambiguity in a criminal statute must be interpreted in defendant's favor.

Notice that these headings are full sentences. They are also framed as assertions, not questions.

The Argument

This section of a legal memorandum is composed of the various arguments. Like the Analysis section in a memorandum or the Explanation section in a client letter, it is the heart and soul of the brief.

In general, there are five types of arguments, each representing a type of authority available to the problem-solver/advocate: text, intent, precedent, tradition, and policy.[7] Text arguments are based on the actual language used in the particular document—e.g., a constitution, statute, administrative rule, or contract. The primary methods for developing text arguments involve plain meaning and the canons of statutory construction.[8]

Intent arguments focus on what the drafters of the document intended by the words they used. Often, intent arguments are paired with text arguments. Thus, in interpreting a Constitutional provision, the advocate looks to the framers' intent; similarly, when interpreting a statute, the advocate looks to the legislature's intent.

Precedent arguments focus on the evolution of the law through judicial opinions. The United States, you will recall, is fundamentally a common law system. In the absence of a controlling statute, courts give great deference to prior courts' opinions. Even when there is a statute, courts will look to how other courts have interpreted and applied that statute.

Tradition arguments are somewhat elusive because they are not based on enacted law or judicial opinions, but on recognized traditions—or fundamental beliefs—that inform our way of life. In business, these types of arguments are based on the ways and customs in which businesses traditionally conduct their affairs.

---

[7] This discussion of the types of arguments draws heavily from Wilson R. Huhn, *Teaching Legal Analysis Using a Pluralistic Model of Law*, 36 Gonzaga L. Rev. 433 (2000-2001).

[8] A more detailed discussion of plain meaning, canons of construction, and legislative intent is provided in Chapter 7.

Policy arguments look at the potential consequences of a proposed rule, interpretation, or outcome. Those consequences are then balanced against the values or policies the law was designed to protect. It is not uncommon for each side to have a policy argument and the court must choose between competing policies. Additionally, policy arguments can be emotionally and politically charged.

Conclusion

The conclusion is a succinct summary and request for relief. Do not try to summarize all the arguments. Instead, state the relief requested and the primary reasons why the relief should be granted.

A Strategy for Getting Started

Beginning a brief can be daunting. These four steps will help you to begin the process of writing.

First, become thoroughly familiar with the record facts. Draw a three-column chart, listing favorable facts, neutral facts, and unfavorable facts.[9]

Second, develop working major and minor point headings. These can be drafted while you are researching and developing your strategy. Do not get overly attached to your initial drafts. They are merely starting points. You will revise and refine them as you revise and refine your arguments.

Third, annotate your working drafts of the point headings. Under each point heading, list the relevant authorities and how you intend to use them. Additionally, list the key points that you intend to make. Finally, list the facts or evidence on which you will rely.

Fourth, select one point heading that relates to a discrete argument and its corresponding annotations and start writing a first draft of the argument. Once you have completed a first draft of that argument, select another point heading and repeat the process.

---

[9] The authors thank UDM Professors Cara Cunningham and Michelle Streicher for this exercise.

This strategy allows you to divide up your writing into manageable units. It is simply not feasible to sit down a write a brief from beginning to end in one sitting unless, perhaps, you have a single issue and a single argument for that issue.

Sample District Court Motion Documents

The following is a template you might use, employing versions of the IRAC structure to advocate how the court should interpret a provision in the federal False Claims Act. The citations in this template generally conform to *The Bluebook*.

For purposes of the sample brief, assume that the lawyer writing it has been presented with the following problem.

> The lawyer's best client is Commonwealth Hospital ("Commonwealth" or "the Hospital"), located in Boom Town, Massachusetts. The Hospital treats patients whose costs are covered by private insurance and patients whose costs are covered by Medicare. In the case of the latter patients, the Hospital bills the federal government according to regulations established by the federal Department of Health and Human Services. The regulations require hospitals to bill the government only for (a) necessary services and procedures that (b) are actually provided. The regulations set a maximum fee for each service or medical procedure. The maximum fee is generally considerably lower than what the Hospital charges its private patients for the same service or procedure.

> Unlike most hospitals, which usually rely on independent physicians, Commonwealth employs several of the surgeons who have privileges at the Hospital. Dr. Marcia Wellford ("Wellford") is one such employed surgeon. Over the years, Wellford and John Smith ("Smith"), who works in the Hospital billing department, have been growing quite uneasy about the Hospital's Medicare billing procedures. For the last three years, they have been secretly making copies at random of surgical and billing records relating to procedures

performed on Medicare patients by employed surgeons. After examining the records, Wellford and Smith concluded that the Hospital consistently has been billing the government for procedures that were either unnecessary or never performed as reported. Wellford and Smith presumed that the billing is intentional and that the purpose and effect are to evade the fee limits and overcharge the government. Wellford and Smith concluded that the Hospital is committing fraud in violation of 31 U.S.C. § 3729, also known as the federal False Claims Act.

While Wellford and Smith have been mulling over what to do with their discoveries, the *Boom Town Dispatch*, the local newspaper, published a lengthy expose of local hospital billing practices. The article included a detailed discussion of Commonwealth's billing of Medicare, quoting a number of unnamed sources as alleging that the Hospital has routinely over billed the government. The sources gave specific alleged examples. The reporter who wrote the article has signed an affidavit that Wellford and Smith were *not* among the sources.

Shortly after the *Dispatch* story was published, and without having first notified the government of their information or intentions, Wellford and Smith brought an action under seal in federal district court in Boom Town. They sued the Hospital under 31 U.S.C. § 3730, the Qui Tam provision in the False Claims Act, which allows individuals with knowledge of fraud on the government to sue on behalf of the government. They complied with 31 U.S.C. § 3730(b)(2) when filing their complaint. The government, pursuant to 31 U.S.C. § 3730(b)(4)(B), declined to take over the action, leaving Wellford and Smith free to go forward as "relators."

The above facts were described in Wellford and Smith's Complaint. The court unsealed the lawsuit and it is pending before Judge Judith Williams in the United States District Court for the District of Massachusetts. The case is entitled *United States ex rel. Marcia Wellford and John Smith v. Commonwealth Hospital, Inc.*, No. Civ. 02-65432 (JW).

Although the Hospital has adamantly denied any wrongdoing, and is planning a vigorous defense, it takes the Complaint allegations at face value for purposes of this pre-answer motion to dismiss under Fed. R. Civ. P. 12(b)(1) for lack of federal subject matter jurisdiction.

**UNITED STATES DISTRICT COURT
FOR THE DISTRICT OF MASSACHUSETTS**

UNITED STATES EX REL. MARCIA WELLFORD AND JOHN SMITH, Plaintiffs, v. COMMONWEALTH HOSPITAL, INC., Defendant.	Case No. Civ. 02-65432 (JW) NOTICE OF MOTION AND MOTION TO DISMISS COMPLAINT	Case caption, including court, names of parties, case number, and document title.

TO: Plaintiff United States of America ex rel. Marcia Wellford and John Smith, and its counsel, Robert Ort, 13 Main Street, Suite 110, Boom Town, Massachusetts 01000.

Notice to other party(ies) in the case and its/their counsel.

PLEASE TAKE NOTICE that at 10:00 a.m. on [Month/Day/20xx], or as soon thereafter as counsel may be heard, Defendant will bring a Motion to Dismiss for hearing before the Honorable Judith Williams, United States District Judge, in Courtroom No. 1, fourth floor, United States Courthouse, 412 Main Street, Boom Town, Massachusetts.

Description line for the day, time, and location of the relevant hearing, and for the type of motion involved.

This Motion is made pursuant to Fed. R. Civ. P. 12(b)(1). The Court lacks subject matter jurisdiction over Plaintiff's complaint because it is based upon allegations that have previously been publicly disclosed within the meaning of 31 U.S.C. § 3730(e)(4)(A).

Summary description of the basis for the motion, including a citation to the relevant procedural rule and substantive statute.

This Motion is made on the basis of the pleadings of the Parties, and the accompanying Memorandum and Affidavits in Support of the Motion.	A standard recitation of the items to which the court should refer in considering the motion.
Dated: March 1, 2003	The date of the notice. The name, attorney registration number, address, and telephone number of the lawyer bringing the motion, along with her signature, and the name of the moving party.

Dated: March 1, 2003

Eve Johnson, #87623
Matters & Johnson
25 Winner Way
Boom Town, MA 01000
(617) 123-4567

Eve Johnson

Attorneys for
Commonwealth
Hospital, Inc.

UNITED STATES DISTRICT COURT
FOR THE DISTRICT OF MASSACHUSETTS

UNITED STATES EX REL.
MARCIA WELLFORD AND Case No.
JOHN SMITH, Civ. 02-65432 (JW)
      Plaintiffs,

v.

COMMONWEALTH AFFIDAVIT OF
HOSPITAL, INC., LUCY SUMMER
      Defendant.

Lucy Summer, being first duly sworn, states as follows:

1. I am the Chief Medical Officer at Commonwealth Hospital, Inc. ("Commonwealth") in Boom Town, Massachusetts.

2. I have been the Chief Medical Officer for the last five years.

3. I submit this affidavit in support of Defendant's motion to dismiss the Plaintiff's complaint for lack of jurisdiction.

4. Dr. Marcia Wellford is an employed surgeon at Commonwealth. Mr. John Smith is a billing clerk at Commonwealth. Because of the confidentiality of the patient names and health information in the medical and billing records at Commonwealth, neither Doctor Wellford nor Mr. Smith is authorized to make copies of records for their own use.

Dated: [Month/Day/20xx] *Lucy Summer*

Notary Public stamp and signature.

Side annotations:

Case caption, including court, names of parties, case number, and document title.

Provide a recitation that the witness is under oath.

Provide background declarations that establish the witness's qualifications to testify.

Provide a recitation of the purpose of the affidavit.

Provide whatever substantive declarations the witness needs to make.

The date and the witness's signature. The Notary attests that the witness swore to the statements in the Notary's presence.

**UNITED STATES DISTRICT COURT
FOR THE DISTRICT OF MASSACHUSETTS**

UNITED STATES EX REL.
MARCIA WELLFORD AND
JOHN SMITH,
          Plaintiffs,
 	
v.
 	
COMMONWEALTH
HOSPITAL, INC.,
          Defendant.
	Case No.
	Civ. 02-65432 (JW)
	
	AFFIDAVIT OF
	SANDY ANDREWS
		(See the margin
		notes on the
		previous page.)

Sandy Andrews, being first duly sworn, states as follows:

1. I am a reporter for the *Boom Town Dispatch*. I have been a reporter for the *Dispatch* since 1996.

2. I submit this affidavit in connection with the motion of Commonwealth Hospital to dismiss plaintiff's complaint.

3. Attached to this affidavit as Exhibit One is a true and correct copy of a newspaper article that I authored and that appeared in the *Boom Town Dispatch* on [Month/Day/20xx.]

4. I interviewed a number of sources for my article. I did not interview Dr. Marcia Wellford or Mr. John Smith, and did not otherwise obtain information from them.

Dated: [Month/Day/20xx]   *Sandy Andrews*

Notary Public stamp and signature

[Authors' Note: In a real case, the newspaper article would be marked and attached as Exhibit One.]

UNITED STATES DISTRICT COURT
FOR THE DISTRICT OF MASSACHUSETTS

UNITED STATES EX REL.
MARCIA WELLFORD AND   Case No.
JOHN SMITH,   Civ. 02-65432 (JW)
            Plaintiff,

v.

COMMONWEALTH
HOSPITAL, INC.,
            Defendant.

**MEMORANDUM IN SUPPORT OF DEFENDANT'S
MOTION TO DISMISS**

INTRODUCTION

The Defendant, Commonwealth Hospital, Inc. ("Commonwealth" or "the Hospital"), submits this Memorandum in support of its Motion to Dismiss Plaintiff's Complaint under Fed. R. Civ. P. 12(b)(1).

In this case, Dr. Marcia Wellford and Mr. John Smith ("Wellford and Smith") allege as relators on behalf of the United States that Commonwealth has committed fraud in billing the federal government for services and procedures for Medicare patients. Commonwealth asks the Court to strike the Complaint on the ground that the allegations in it are based upon newspaper reports of the same alleged information. Thus, Wellford and Smith are not proper relators within the meaning of the federal False Claims Act, 31 U.S.C. §§ 3729, 3730 (2000).

**UNDISPUTED FACTS AND
PROCEDURAL POSTURE**

For purposes of this Motion, the following matters are undisputed:

Case caption, including court, names of parties, case number, and document title.

Provide a succinct introductory section that tells the court what the case is about, what the motion is about, what the party's position is on the motion, and what relief the party requests.

In this section, provide a description of the key facts and procedural posture that will drive the result, with detailed cites to the record for the convenience of

Commonwealth is located in Boom Town, Massachusetts. Plaintiff's Complaint ("Pl.'s Compl.") ¶ 3 (Month Day, 20xx). The Hospital treats patients whose costs are covered by private insurance and patients whose costs are covered by Medicare. *Id.* at ¶ 4. In the case of the latter patients, the Hospital bills the federal government according to regulations established by the federal Department of Health and Human Services. *Id.* The regulations require hospitals to bill the government only for (a) necessary services and procedures that (b) are actually provided. *Id.* at ¶ 5. The regulations set a maximum fee for each service or medical procedure. *Id.* at ¶ 6. The maximum fee is generally lower than what the Hospital charges its private patients for the same service or procedure. *Id.*

Unlike most hospitals, which usually rely on independent physicians, Commonwealth employs several of the surgeons who have privileges at the Hospital. *Id.* at ¶ 10. Wellford is one such employed surgeon. *Id.* at ¶ 2; Affidavit of Lucy Summers ("Aff. Summers") ¶ 4. Commonwealth also employs billing personnel, one of whom is Smith. *Id.* For the last three years, Wellford and Smith have been secretly making copies at random of surgical and billing records relating to procedures performed on Medicare patients by employed surgeons at Commonwealth. Pl.'s Compl. at ¶ 13. The copying was unauthorized and violates patient confidentiality. Aff. Summers ¶ 4.

After examining the records, Wellford and Smith concluded that the Hospital was billing the government for procedures that were either unnecessary or never performed as reported. Pl.'s Compl. at ¶ 15. Wellford and Smith presumed that the billing was intentional and that the purpose and effect were to evade the fee limits and overcharge the government. *Id.* at ¶ 16. Wellford and Smith further presumed that the Hospital was committing fraud in violation of 31 U.S.C. § 3729, also known as the federal False Claims Act. *Id.* at ¶ 17.

Prior to the filing of the present lawsuit, the *Boom Town Dispatch*, the local newspaper, published a lengthy article concerning the billing practices of a number of area hospitals, including Commonwealth. *Id.* at ¶ 18; Affidavit of Sandy

---

the Court and to establish credibility. The description can and should be worded so as to put the client's best foot forward, but must be accurate.

Note that there will be trial court briefs you will write from time to time where the facts are disputed. But in the present example, defense counsel wants to focus on undisputed facts to bolster the defense position that the case may be summarily and easily dismissed.

Strictly speaking for purposes of the present motion, this is an irrelevant point. But defense counsel may still choose to point it out, to take away some of the luster that might otherwise attach to Wellford and Smith as defenders of the public.

The fact description must cover the handful of key facts that drive the legal outcome from the standpoint of the writer. The existence of a prior newspaper

Andrews ("Aff. Andrews") ¶ 3, Ex. One. The article included a detailed discussion of Commonwealth's billing of Medicare. Aff. Andrews at ¶ 3, Ex. One. The article quoted a number of unnamed sources as alleging that the Hospital has routinely over billed the government. *Id.* The sources claimed to identify specific examples. *Id.* The reporter who wrote the article has signed an affidavit that Wellford and Smith were *not* among the sources. Aff. Andrews at ¶ 4. Plaintiff's Complaint allegations mirror the *Dispatch* article's content.

Shortly after the *Dispatch* story was published, and without having first notified the government of their information or intentions, Wellford and Smith brought an action under seal in federal district court in Boom Town. Pl.'s Compl. at ¶ 19. They sued the Hospital under 31 U.S.C. § 3730, the Qui Tam provision in the False Claims Act, which allows individuals with knowledge of fraud on the government to sue on behalf of the government. *Id.* at ¶ 1. They complied with 31 U.S.C. § 3730(b)(2) when filing their complaint. *Id.* at ¶ 20. The government, pursuant to 31 U.S.C. § 3730(b)(4)(B), declined to take over the action, leaving Wellford and Smith free to go forward as "relators."

Although the Hospital has adamantly denied any wrongdoing and is planning a vigorous defense, its position for present purposes is simply that, taking the above information as given, the Court should dismiss the Complaint under Fed. R. Civ. P. 12(b)(1) for lack of federal subject matter jurisdiction.

ARGUMENT

I. **PLAINTIFF HAS THE BURDEN OF ESTABLISHING SUBJECT MATTER JURISDICTION OVER THE COMPLAINT.**

Federal courts have limited jurisdiction. *United States ex rel. Precision Co. v. Koch Indus. Inc.*, 971 F.2d 548, 551 (10th Cir. 1992). If the defendant contests subject matter jurisdiction, the plaintiff must come forward with competent proof that jurisdiction exists. *Id.* If the Plaintiff in the present case cannot establish jurisdiction, this Court should dismiss the Complaint.

---

article containing similar allegations in detail is one such key fact.

The fact that Wellford and Smith did not provide information to the government prior to filing their lawsuit is a second key fact from the Defendant's perspective. The fact that the United States Attorney General is not bringing the case is the third key fact from the Defendant's perspective.

Conservative lawyers often insert some form of rejection of the other side's allegations into pleadings and motion papers to protect the record in case the litigation continues to go forward.

The first discussion in a typical memorandum is the relevant burden of proof on the instant issue.

II.   AS A MATTER OF LAW, PLAINTIFF CANNOT ESTABLISH SUBJECT MATTER JURISDICTION OVER THE COMPLAINT IN THIS CASE.

The subject matter jurisdiction provision in the federal False Claims Act provides:

> (A) *No court shall have jurisdiction* over an action under this section *based upon* the *public disclosure* of allegations or transactions . . . from the *news media, unless* the action is brought by the Attorney General or the person bringing the action is an *original source* of the information. (B) For purposes of this paragraph, "original source" means an individual who has direct and independent knowledge of the information on which the allegations are based *and* has voluntarily *provided* the information to the Government *before filing* an action under this section which is based on the information.

31 U.S.C. § 3730(e)(4) (emphasis supplied).

When a defendant contests jurisdiction under this provision in a case not brought by the Attorney General, the court must make three inquiries:

1. Has there been a public disclosure of the relevant allegations;

2. If yes, does the relator who brings the suit on behalf of the government base his or her claims upon the public disclosure; and

3. If yes, then is the relator an "original source" of the information within the meaning of the statute?

United States ex rel. O'Keeffe v. Sverdup Corp., 131 F. Supp. 2d 87, 91 (D. Mass. 2001).

The major point heading introduces the argument for the specific issue before the court. (If there is more than one issue, then you will have a major point heading for each issue.)

Provide the relevant rule. If the rule arises from enacted law, then begin with a quotation of the material provisions of the law. (If the rule is from the common law, then provide a statement of the rule and an appropriate citation.)

Break out the separate elements of the rule.

Two of these elements are undisputed and indisputable in the present case: The allegations that Wellford and Smith have made against Commonwealth also have been made in a newspaper report that pre-dates the filing of the Complaint. And Wellford and Smith are not "original sources" within the meaning of § 3730(e)(4)(B), because they did not provide their information to the government before they filed their Complaint. Accordingly, if the Complaint is "based upon" the newspaper article, there is no subject matter jurisdiction.

Tell the Court which elements are actually in dispute, and focus the Court's attention on the issue that the rest of the brief will address, to resolve the problem.

A. "Based upon" means "the same as" or "substantially similar to" the allegations in the newspaper.

The most recent case in this District has held that a complaint is "based upon" prior public disclosures within the meaning of 31 U.S.C. § 3730(e)(4) if the complaint allegations are "similar to or the same as those that have been publicly disclosed." *O'Keeffe*, 131 F. Supp. 2d at 92. This is also the view of the vast majority of federal circuit courts. *United States ex rel. Minn. Ass'n of Nurse Anesthetists v. Allina Health Sys. Corp.*, 276 F.3d. 1032, 1044-47 (8th Cir. 2002); *United States ex rel. Mistick PBT v. Hous. Auth. of Pittsburgh*, 186 F.3d 376, 386-88 (3d Cir. 1999); *United States ex rel. Biddle v. Bd. of Trustees of Leland Stanford Jr. Univ.*, 161 F.3d 533, 536-40 (9th Cir. 1998); *United States ex rel. McKenzie v. BellSouth Telecomm., Inc.*, 123 F.3d 935, 940-41 (6th Cir. 1997); *United States ex rel. Findley v. FPC-Boron Employees' Club*, 105 F.3d 675, 682-85 (D.C. Cir. 1997); *Cooper v. Blue Cross and Blue Shield of Fla., Inc.*, 19 F.3d 562, 566-67 (11th Cir. 1994); *Precision Co.*, 971 F.2d at 552-53; *United States ex rel. Doe v. John Doe Corp.*, 960 F.2d 318, 324 (2d Cir. 1992). The First Circuit has not yet taken a position.

Start with a sub-heading that states your own high ground. Note that in this sample, the entire section (A) is used to develop the rule section.

Start with favorable authority from your own jurisdiction.

Often, string-citing merely persuasive authority from other jurisdictions is not the best use of precious space and time. However, in the present case involving an unsettled matter of law, a "weight of the authority" argument can be useful.

This District in *O'Keeffe* correctly summarized the two primary reasons why "based upon" means "similar to or the same." First, the public disclosure jurisdictional bar was adopted by Congress in 1986 as part of a complex balancing of competing public interests. On the one hand, Congress wanted to provide whistleblowers with incentives to come forward with valuable information concerning fraud upon the government. On the other hand, Congress sought to discourage mere

Explain the policy bases for the relevant legal rule.

parasitical suits based upon information already in the possession of federal authorities. 131 F. Supp. 2d at 91 (citing *United States ex rel. Springfield Terminal Ry. Co. v. Quinn*, 14 F.3d 645, 649 (D.C. Cir. 1994)). There is no reason to reward relators for providing information that is the same or similar to allegations already published. *O'Keeffe*, 131 F. Supp. 2d at 93 (citing *Findley*, 105 F.3d at 685).

Second, if "based upon" means only "derived from" (which is the alternative construction of the term typically proposed by plaintiffs), then the "original source" requirement in § 3730(e)(4) is rendered superfluous. By definition, if a relator's allegations are not derived from prior public disclosures, the relator has direct and independent knowledge of his claims. *O'Keeffe*, 131 F. Supp. 2d at 93. Thus, a separate original source requirement is unnecessary. But a standard rule of statutory construction is that a statute should be construed so as not to render any of its terms superfluous. *United States v. Nordic Village, Inc.*, 503 U.S. 30, 36 (1992). Thus, the fact that Congress thought it necessary to write an original source exception into § 3730(e)(4) must mean that Congress intended a broader view of the term "based upon" than simply "derived from." *O'Keeffe*, 131 F. Supp. 2d at 93.

> Employ principles of statutory construction.

In *O'Keeffe*, the plaintiff alleged that the defendants had falsified the results of an engineering study of the environmental impact of the proposed restoration of commuter rail service in Southeastern Massachusetts. Because both the allegedly false facts and the allegedly true facts were publicly disclosed in the documents and hearings relating to the rail project, this District ruled that the complaint was "based upon" the prior public disclosures, and granted summary judgment for the defense when plaintiff could not establish that he was an original source of the relevant information. 131 F. Supp. 2d at 96-100.

> Outline the facts in the key case and, if material, synthesize the patterns in the facts across the group of cases on which you rely.

B. This Court is not bound by the limited precedent that defines "based upon" as "derived from."

Wellford and Smith asserted in a pre-trial conference that the present Complaint is not derived from the *Boom Town*

> Even though you may have a reply brief, and might conclude that you should withhold your discussion of the adverse authorities to that reply, the authors recommend that you inoculate the court

Dispatch newspaper article, and that because the allegations are not so derived, this Court has subject matter jurisdiction. Further, Wellford and Smith ostensibly rely on two prior decisions of this Court. *United States ex rel. LeBlanc v. Raytheon Co.*, 874 F. Supp. 35, 41 (D. Mass. 1995), *aff'd*, 62 F.3d 1411 (1st Cir. 1995); *United States ex rel. LaValley v. First Nat'l Bank of Boston*, 707 F. Supp. 1351, 1367 (D. Mass. 1988). Wellford and Smith also seemingly rely on the two federal circuit court opinions that have adopted the "derived from" construction of § 3730(e)(4). *United States v. Bank of Farmington*, 166 F.3d 853, 863 (7th Cir. 1999); *United States ex rel. Siller v. Becton Dickinson & Co.*, 21 F.3d 1339, 1348 (4th Cir. 1994). But none of these cases controls the present one.

In *LaValley*, the court first had to decide whether the 1986 False Claims Act amendments that resulted in 31 U.S.C. § 3730(e)(4)(A) and (B) should even apply retroactively to a case filed in 1985. The vast majority of the court's opinion was devoted to that question. When the court did reach the "based upon" definitional issue, it did so without the benefit of any of the later circuit court precedent.

In *LeBlanc*, the court stated that it did not matter whether the plaintiff's allegations were derived from or merely similar to the prior public disclosures in the case, because LeBlanc failed to establish subject matter jurisdiction under either test. Thus, the court's preference for one definition over the other was dictum. And, because the First Circuit's affirmance was an unpublished, summary one, the fact of the affirmance is of no precedential value in the present case. *See* 1st Cir. R. 36(c), 32.3.

Similarly, Wellford and Smith can place no reliance upon the *Bank of Farmington* case because a different panel of the Seventh Circuit more or less simultaneously concluded that, when the allegations of a whistleblower plaintiff have been previously publicly disclosed, the court has jurisdiction "only if" the plaintiff is an "original source" of the facts. *United States ex rel. Lamers v. City of Green Bay*, 168 F.3d 1013, 1017 (7th Cir. 1999). The viability of the *Bank of Farmington* opinion is questionable even in the court that rendered it.

against the adverse authorities in this opening brief. This recommendation particularly holds true in the present case, where two of the adverse authorities are from your own jurisdiction (and thus you have an obligation as an officer of the court to cite them), and the two other adverse authorities are so obvious that you are not tipping off opposing counsel to anything they will not find anyway.

Go through the authorities and argue that they can be ignored, and/or that they can be distinguished, and/or that they are actually helpful, and/or that they are simply wrongly decided.

Note that in this sample, the entire section (B) is devoted to a counterargument, which has been inserted as a continuation of the rule section.

That only leaves the Fourth Circuit's opinion in *Siller*. But *Siller* is not binding upon this Court. Moreover, its logic has been rejected by the Second, Third, Sixth, Eighth, Ninth, Tenth, Eleventh, and D.C. Circuits, as well as implicitly by a panel of the Seventh Circuit. The *Siller* court's "derived from" construction of the term "based upon" is inconsistent with the federal courts' limited jurisdiction: It is inconsistent with Congress' decision not to create whistleblower standing for would-be plaintiffs who give the government information the government already has; and it is inconsistent with the "original source" provision in the statute.

C. Plaintiff's Complaint in this matter is "based upon" the prior *Boom Town Dispatch* newspaper article.

It is undisputed that the *Boom Town Dispatch* on [Month/Day/20xx] published an article concerning the billing practices of various area hospitals, including Commonwealth. Pl.'s Compl. At ¶ 18; Aff. Andrews ¶ 3, Ex. One. It is also undisputed that the article included a detailed discussion of Commonwealth's billing of Medicare. Aff. Andrews ¶ 3, Ex. One. The article identified specific alleged examples of fraudulent billing practices. *Id.* A simple facial comparison of Wellford and Smith's Complaint with the article reveals that the allegations mirror each other. Thus, by definition, Wellford and Smith's Complaint is the same as, or similar to, the publicly disclosed allegations in the newspaper article. This similarity means, as a matter of law, that the Court lacks subject matter jurisdiction in this case, as Wellford and Smith are not proper plaintiffs under the federal False Claims Act.

> Apply the rule to the instant facts. Note that in this sample, the application is set out in a separate section. Compare the use of the IRAC formula in the Appellate Brief template.

CONCLUSION

This Court should grant Commonwealth's motion to dismiss the Complaint for lack of subject matter jurisdiction under Fed. R. Civ. P. 12(b)(1). If the United States believed there was good reason to pursue a claim against Commonwealth, it could have done so through the Attorney General in the manner described by the False Claims Act. But the United States did not pursue the case. Instead, Wellford and Smith are pursuing the case in the government's name. This

> Provide a formal conclusion, requesting relief.

they cannot do, for their allegations are based upon prior public disclosures within the meaning of 31 U.S.C. § 3730(e)(4).

Dated: March 1, 2003   Respectfully submitted,

                                        Eve Johnson, #87623
                                        Matters & Johnson
                                        25 Winner Way
                                        Boom Town, MA. 01000
                                        (617) 123-4567

                                        Eve Johnson
                                        Attorneys for
                                        Commonwealth Hospital,
                                        Inc.

UNITED STATES DISTRICT COURT
FOR THE DISTRICT OF MASSACHUSETTS

UNITED STATES EX REL.
MARCIA WELLFORD AND   Case No.
JOHN SMITH,   Civ. 02-65432 (JW)
        Plaintiffs,

v.

COMMONWEALTH   [Defendant's Proposed]
HOSPITAL, INC.,   Findings of Fact
        Defendant.   and Conclusions of Law

The local rules in many district courts require counsel to submit proposed orders as part of their motion papers. Fed. R. Civ. P. 52 requires federal district courts to enter findings of fact and conclusions of law when they decide various matters.

This matter came on for hearing before the Honorable Judith Williams on [Month/Day/20xx] at the United States Courthouse, Boom Town, Massachusetts.

Robert Ort appeared on behalf of Plaintiff. Eve Johnson appeared on behalf of Defendant.

Now, therefore, upon all of the files, records, proceedings, and arguments of counsel, the Court makes the following:

Note how closely the proposed findings and conclusions mirror the Hospital's brief.

FINDINGS OF FACT

1. Commonwealth is located in Boom Town, Massachusetts. Plaintiff's Complaint ("Pl.'s Compl.") ¶ 3 (Month Day, 20xx.)
2. The Hospital treats both patients whose costs are covered by private insurance and patients whose costs are covered by Medicare. *Id.* at ¶ 4.
3. In the case of the latter patients, the Hospital bills the federal government according to regulations established by the federal Department of Health and Human Services. *Id.*
4. The regulations require hospitals to bill the government only for (a) necessary services and procedures that (b) are actually provided. *Id.* at ¶ 5.
5. The regulations set a maximum fee for each service or

medical procedure. _Id._ at ¶ 6.

    6. The maximum fee is generally lower than what the hospital charges its private patients for the same service or procedure. _Id._

    7. Unlike most hospitals, which usually rely on independent physicians, Commonwealth employs several of the surgeons who have privileges at the Hospital. _Id._ at ¶ 10.

    8. Dr. Marcia Wellford is one such employed surgeon. _Id._ at ¶ 2; Affidavit of Lucy Summers ("Aff. Summers") at ¶ 4.

    9. Commonwealth also employs billing personnel, one of whom is Mr. John Smith. _Id._

    10. For the last three years, Wellford and Smith have been secretly making copies at random of surgical and billing records relating to procedures performed on Medicare patients by employed surgeons at Commonwealth. Pl.'s Compl. at ¶ 13.

    11. After examining the records, Wellford and Smith have accused the Hospital of billing the government for procedures that were either unnecessary or were actually never performed as reported. Pl.'s Compl. at ¶ 15.

    12. Wellford and Smith presume that the billing is intentional, and that the purpose and effect are to evade the fee limits and to overcharge the government. _Id._ at ¶ 16.

    13. Wellford and Smith assert that the Hospital is committing fraud in violation of 31 U.S.C. § 3729, also known as the federal False Claims Act. _Id._ at ¶ 17.

    14. Prior to the filing of the present lawsuit, the _Boom Town Dispatch_, the local newspaper, published a lengthy article concerning the billing practices of a number of area hospitals, including Commonwealth. _Id._ at ¶ 18; Affidavit of Sandy Andrews ("Aff. Andrews") at ¶ 3, Ex. One.

    15. The article included a detailed discussion of Commonwealth's billing of Medicare. Aff. Andrews ¶ 3, Ex. One.

    16. The article quoted a number of unnamed sources as alleging that the Hospital has routinely over billed the government. _Id._

    17. The sources claimed to identify specific examples. _Id._

    18. The reporter who wrote the article has signed an affidavit that Wellford and Smith were _not_ among the sources. Aff. Andrews at ¶ 4.

    19. A side-by-side comparison reveals that Plaintiff's Complaint allegations mirror the _Dispatch_ article's content.

    20. Shortly after the _Dispatch_ story was published, and

without having first notified the government of their information or intentions, Wellford and Smith brought an action under seal in this federal district court. Pl.'s Compl. at ¶ 19.

21. They sued the Hospital under 31 U.S.C. § 3730, the Qui Tam provision in the False Claims Act, which allows individuals with knowledge of fraud on the government to sue on behalf of the government. *Id.* at ¶ 1.

22. They complied with 31 U.S.C. § 3730(b)(2) when filing their complaint. *Id.* at ¶ 20.

23. The government, pursuant to 31 U.S.C. § 3730(b)(4)(B), declined to take over the action, leaving Wellford and Smith free to go forward as relators.

CONCLUSIONS OF LAW

1. Federal courts have limited jurisdiction. *United States ex rel. Precision Co. v. Koch Indus. Inc.*, 971 F.2d 548, 551 (10th Cir. 1992). If the defendant contests subject matter jurisdiction, the plaintiff must come forward with competent proof that jurisdiction exists. *Id.* If the Plaintiff in the present case cannot establish jurisdiction, this Court should dismiss the Complaint.

2. The subject matter jurisdiction provision in the federal False Claims Act states as follows:

> (A) *No court shall have jurisdiction* over an action under this section *based upon* the *public disclosure* of allegations or transactions . . . from the *news media, unless* the action is brought by the Attorney General or the person bringing the action is an *original source* of the information. (B) For purposes of this paragraph, 'original source' means an individual who has direct and independent knowledge of the information on which the allegations are based *and* has voluntarily *provided* the information to the Government *before filing* an action under this section which is based on the information.

31 U.S.C. § 3730(e)(4) (emphasis supplied.)

3. When a defendant contests jurisdiction under this provision in a case not brought by the Attorney General, the court must make three inquiries:

First, has there been a public disclosure of the relevant allegations;

Second, if yes, does the relator who brings the suit on behalf of the government base his or her claims upon the public disclosure; and

Third, if yes, then is the relator an "original source" of the information within the meaning of the statute?

United States ex rel. O'Keeffe v. Sverdup Corp., 131 F. Supp. 2d 87, 91 (D. Mass. 2001).

4. Two of these elements are undisputed and indisputable in the present case: The allegations that Wellford and Smith have made against Commonwealth also have been made in a newspaper report that pre-dates the filing of the Complaint. And Wellford and Smith are not "original sources" within the meaning of § 3730(e)(4)(B), because they did not provide their information to the Government before they filed their Complaint. Accordingly, if the Complaint is "based upon" the newspaper article, there is no subject matter jurisdiction.

5. The most recent case in this District has held that a complaint is "based upon" prior public disclosures within the meaning of 31 U.S.C. § 3730(e)(4) if the complaint allegations are "similar to or the same as those that have been publicly disclosed." *O'Keeffe*, 131 F. Supp. 2d at 92. This is also the view of the vast majority of federal circuit courts. *United States ex rel. Minn. Ass'n of Nurse Anesthetists v. Allina Health Sys. Corp.*, 276 F.3d. 1032, 1044-47 (8th Cir. 2002); *United States ex rel. Mistick PBT v. Hous. Auth. of Pittsburgh*, 186 F.3d 376, 386-88 (3d Cir. 1999); *United States ex rel. Biddle v. Bd. of Trustees of Leland Stanford Jr. Univ.*, 161 F.3d 533, 536-40 (9th Cir. 1998); *United States ex rel. McKenzie v. BellSouth Telecomm., Inc.*, 123 F.3d 935, 940-41 (6th Cir. 1997); *United States ex rel. Findley v. FPC-Boron Employees' Club*, 105 F.3d 675, 682-85 (D.C. Cir. 1997); *Cooper v. Blue Cross and Blue Shield of Fla., Inc.*, 19 F.3d 562, 566-67 (11th Cir. 1994); *Precision Co.*, 971 F.2d at 552-53; *United States ex rel. Doe v. John Doe Corp.*, 960 F.2d 318, 324 (2d Cir. 1992). The First Circuit has not yet taken a position.

6. This District in *O'Keeffe* correctly summarized the two primary reasons why "based upon" means "similar to or the same." First, the public disclosure jurisdictional bar was adopted by Congress in 1986 as part of a complex balancing of competing public interests. On the one hand, Congress wanted to provide relators with incentives to come forward with valuable information concerning fraud upon the government. On the other hand, Congress sought to discourage mere parasitical suits based upon information already in the possession of federal authorities. 131 F. Supp. 2d at 91 (citing *United States ex rel. Springfield Terminal Ry. Co. v. Quinn*, 14 F.3d 645, 649 (D.C. Cir. 1994)). There is no reason to reward relators for providing information that is the same or similar to allegations already published. *O'Keeffe,* 131 F. Supp. 2d at 93, citing *Findley*, 105 F.3d at 685.

7. Second, if "based upon" means only "derived from," then the "original source" requirement in § 3730(e)(4) is rendered superfluous. By definition, if a relator's allegations are not derived from prior public disclosures, the relator has direct and independent knowledge of his claims. *O'Keeffe*, 131 F. Supp. 2d at 93. Thus, a separate original source requirement is unnecessary. But a standard rule of statutory construction is that a statute should be construed so as not to render any of its terms superfluous. *United States v. Nordic Village, Inc.*, 503 U.S. 30, 36 (1992). Thus, the fact that Congress thought it necessary to write an original source exception into § 3730(e)(4) must mean that Congress intended a broader view of the term "based upon" than simply "derived from." *O'Keeffe*, 131 F. Supp. 2d at 93.

8. Wellford and Smith argue that the present Complaint is not derived from the *Boom Town Dispatch* newspaper article, and that because the allegations are not so derived, this Court has subject matter jurisdiction. Wellford and Smith necessarily rely on two prior decisions of this Court. *United States ex rel. LeBlanc v. Raytheon Co.,* 874 F. Supp. 35, 41 (D. Mass. 1995), *aff'd*, 62 F.3d 1411 (1st Cir. 1995); *United States ex rel. LaValley v. First Nat'l Bank of Boston*, 707 F. Supp. 1351, 1367 (D. Mass. 1988). Wellford and Smith also rely on the two federal circuit court opinions in which the courts adopted the "derived from" construction of § 3730(e)(4). *United States v. Bank of Farmington*, 166 F.3d 853, 863 (7th Cir. 1999*); United States ex rel. Siller v. Becton Dickinson & Co.*, 21 F.3d 1339, 1348 (4th Cir. 1994).

None of these cases controls the present one.

    9. This Court grants Commonwealth's Motion to Dismiss the Complaint for lack of subject matter jurisdiction under Fed. R. Civ. P. 12(b)(1). If the United States believed there was good reason to pursue a claim against Commonwealth, it could have done so through the Attorney General in the manner described in the False Claims Act. But the United States did not pursue the case. Instead, Wellford and Smith are pursuing the case in the government's name. This they cannot do, for their allegations are based upon prior public disclosures within the meaning of 31 U.S.C. § 3730(e)(4).

    LET JUDGMENT BE ENTERED ACCORDINGLY IN FAVOR OF THE DEFENDANT.

Dated: [Month/Day/20xx]

                                      _____
                                    United States District Judge

[Note: Under the local rules of the District of Massachusetts, court documents would be double-spaced, except for certain items such as footnotes. We single-spaced the models to save space.]

THE APPELLATE BRIEF
TEMPLATE

How would you prepare an appellate brief on this issue, employing the IRAC organizational formula? A basic template is provided below in the sample excerpted brief for Appellant Commonwealth Hospital.[10] The citations generally conform to *The Bluebook*. Although we have followed a general format for briefs filed in federal circuit courts, we have, for publication-space-limitation purposes, not followed certain requirements of the Federal Rules of Appellate Procedure. For example, if this brief were filed in the First Circuit, it would have a blue cover (for appellant), the brief would be double-spaced, and the font size would be 14. When you are preparing appellate briefs, either to a federal court or a state court, make sure you follow the appropriate court rules, both the general ones and the local ones. Our principal goal is to provide you with one way to organize a brief on this problem employing the IRAC organizational structure.

In reviewing the sample brief, note that the advocate had to consider *how* to present the arguments. In other words, the advocate had to develop a strategy. Here, the advocate had a number of things to consider. For example, if the appellate court affirms the district court, then the Hospital will be defending a multi-million dollar lawsuit—or attempting to settle—unless the Supreme Court grants certiorari and reverses. But while this is an especially important appeal for the Hospital, counsel very well may conclude that in presenting the arguments, the best strategy is to demonstrate that this is a relatively simple and straightforward statutory construction issue and the great weight of authority—the opinions of other circuit courts—favors the interpretation advocated by the Hospital.[11]

---

[10] For a more in-depth discussion of appellate advocacy and various principles discussed below, see Clary et al., *supra* ch. 1 n.1, at 3-95; Mary Beth Beazley, *A Practical Guide to Appellate Advocacy* (Aspen L. & Bus. 2002).

[11] There are, of course, other strategies. For example, counsel may conclude, and the Hospital may agree, that the most persuasive argument will be to emphasize the legislative history of the False Claims Act through an independent analysis, only using the opinions from other circuits as support. As an academic exercise, a legal writing professor may well expect this type of appellate brief problem to require independent research and analysis of the statute's legislative history, as well as an examination of how other circuits have decided the issue.

Additionally, counsel had to determine how much emphasis to place on the story and how much on the law. On the one hand, the Hospital is in the noble profession of healing the sick. On the other hand, the Hospital has been accused of defrauding the government, which the Hospital denies. Counsel may conclude on appeal that the best strategy is to emphasize the reasoning of other courts, rather than the particular facts of this case or the other cases. This can be a useful strategy with issues of first impression in general, and/or, more specifically, where the law is more favorable than the factual story may be. In other words, the "compare and contrast" analysis in these circumstances may focus on the legal reasoning of the courts in interpreting the relevant language instead of on the facts of the individual cases.

Note also some template differences between an appellate brief and a trial court brief. Appellate briefs typically require special sections such as a table of contents, a table of authorities, a recitation of the jurisdictional grounds for appeal, a formal statement of the facts and procedural posture, and a summary of the argument.

One of the special sections may consist of a specific discussion of the proper standard for the appellate court to employ in reviewing a trial court's conclusions. Normally, an appellate court reviews questions of law *de novo*.[12] But the court typically reviews questions of fact only for clear error (court findings),[13] reasonable basis (jury findings),[14] or substantial evidence (agency findings).[15] And the court normally reviews discretionary matters only for abuse of the discretion.[16] These standards can make a substantial difference in the likelihood of an affirmance or reversal on appeal. Accordingly, appellate courts expect a discussion of the relevant standard for the appeal in question, either as a distinct section of a brief or at the beginning of the argument section.

---

[12] *Bose Corp. v. Consumers Union of United States, Inc.*, 466 U.S. 485, 498 & 501, 104 S. Ct. 1949 (1984).

[13] *United States v. United States Gypsum Co.*, 333 U.S. 364, 395, 68 S. Ct. 525 (1948).

[14] *Lavender v. Kurn*, 327 U.S. 645, 652-53, 66 S. Ct. 740 (1946).

[15] *F.T.C. v. Ind. Fed'n of Dentists*, 476 U.S. 447, 454, 465, 106 S. Ct. 2009 (1986).

[16] *E.g. Gen. Elec. Co. v. Joiner*, 522 U.S. 136, 141, 118 S. Ct. 512 (1997).

Another special section in a typical appellate brief is a formal statement of the issue(s) presented on appeal. This is a stand-alone segment within the brief, not merely a discussion within the narrative introduction found in a typical trial court brief. And the segment may take different forms: It may consist of simple questions. It may instead consist of "whether . . ." statements. It may alternatively be constructed as a short narrative with a question attached. Look for the example and the accompanying margin notes in the sample brief that follows.

For purposes of this sample brief, assume the following additional facts:

After a hearing, the District Court denied the Hospital's Motion to Dismiss. In denying the Motion, the court rejected the analysis in *United States ex rel. O'Keeffe v. Sverdup Corp.,* 131 F. Supp. 2d 87, 91 (D. Mass. 2001), and instead followed the earlier district court opinions in *United States ex rel. LaValley v. First Natl. Bank of Boston,* 707 F. Supp. 1351 (D. Mass. 1988), and *United States ex rel. LeBlanc v. Raytheon Co.,* 874 F. Supp. 35 (D. Mass. 1995). Additionally, the court explicitly adopted the interpretation advanced by the Fourth Circuit in *United States ex rel. Siller v. Becton Dickinson & Co.,* 21 F.3d 1339 (4th Cir. 1994). Recognizing, however, a split within the district, as well as among the circuits, and the lack of an authoritative First Circuit opinion, the court held *sua sponte* that its " 'order involves a controlling question of law as to which there is substantial ground for difference of opinion and that an immediate appeal from the order may materially advance the ultimate termination of the litigation' " (quoting 28 U.S.C. § 1292(b) (2000)) and certified the order for interlocutory appeal. The First Circuit has accepted the appeal.

IN THE UNITED STATES COURT OF APPEALS
FOR THE
FIRST CIRCUIT

NO. 02-XXXX-MASS.

UNITED STATES EX REL.
MARCIA WELLFORD AND JOHN SMITH,

Plaintiffs-Appellees,

v.

COMMONWEALTH HOSPITAL, INC.,

Defendant-Appellant.

BRIEF OF APPELLANT
COMMONWEALTH HOSPITAL, INC.

Eve Johnson, #87623
Matters & Johnson
25 Winner Way
Boom Town, MA 01000
(617) 123-4567

ATTORNEY FOR APPELLANT
COMMONWEALTH HOSPITAL, INC.

Robert Ort #98709
13 Main Street, Suite 110
Boom Town, MA 01000
(617) 765-4321

ATTORNEY FOR APPELLEE
UNITED STATES EX REL.
MARCIA WELLFORD AND JOHN SMITH

Margin notes:

Provide the case caption, now with appropriate appellate descriptions.

Ordinarily, when there are only two sets of attorneys to be listed, the names would go side-by-side. However to accommodate these margin notes, we have listed one name over the other.

CORPORATE DISCLOSURE STATEMENT

Commonwealth Hospital has no parent corporation and is not owned by any publicly held company.

This kind of disclosure statement is now required in the federal appellate courts.

TABLE OF CONTENTS	
	Insert the correct page number for each section of the brief. (We have omitted them here because we have not included page numbers in the template.)
CORPORATE DISCLOSURE STATEMENT . . . .[insert page]	
TABLE OF CONTENTS	
TABLE OF AUTHORITIES	
REASONS WHY ORAL ARGUMENT SHOULD BE HEARD	
JURISDICTIONAL STATEMENT	
STATEMENT OF THE ISSUE PRESENTED FOR REVIEW	
STATEMENT OF THE CASE	
A. Overview B. Facts	
SUMMARY OF ARGUMENT	
ARGUMENT	
I. AS A MATTER OF LAW, THE DISTRICT COURT ERRED IN ASSERTING SUBJECT MATTER JURISDICTION IN THE QUI TAM ACTION AGAINST COMMONWEALTH HOSPITAL.	Your argument headings serve as a roadmap.
A. Federal Statutes Conferring Jurisdiction Are Strictly Construed.	
B. The False Claims Act's Jurisdictional Bar Precludes Qui Tam Actions That Are Based on Allegations That Have Been Disclosed Publicly, Unless the Relator Qualifies as an "Original Source."	

1. *"Based upon" means "the same as" or "substantially similar to" information or evidence that has been publicly disclosed.*

2. *Congress intended to limit federal qui tam actions that repeat information the government already possesses.*

C. The District Court Erred in Relying on *Siller* and Asserting Jurisdiction Over This Qui Tam Action.

CONCLUSION

CERTIFICATE OF COMPLIANCE

ADDENDUM

TABLE OF AUTHORITIES

Cases

Bailey v. United States, 516 U.S. 137 (1995) . . . . [insert page]

Statutes

28 U.S.C. § 1292(b) . . . . [insert page]

Rules

Fed. R. Civ. P. 12(b)(1) . . . . [insert page]

Secondary Authorities

The cases are normally listed in alphabetical order. Some courts prefer that you place cases in hierarchical categories (i.e., all U.S. Supreme Court cases first), and then alphabetically within each category.

Statutes and court rules are normally listed in numerical order.

Secondary authorities are normally listed in alphabetical order. (No secondary authorities were used in this template.)

REASONS WHY ORAL ARGUMENT SHOULD BE HEARD

This case involves an issue of first impression, requiring the Court to interpret Section 3730(e)(4) of the False Claims Act. Dr. Marcia Wellford and Mr. John Smith ("Wellford and Smith") allege as relators on behalf of the United States (collectively "Plaintiff-Appellee") that Defendant-Appellant Commonwealth Hospital, Inc. ("Commonwealth" or "the Hospital") has fraudulently billed the federal government for services and procedures on Medicare patients. The government has declined to take over the case or to intervene.

Section 3730(e)(4) requires that relators such as Wellford and Smith not base their allegations on, among other things, previously reported newspaper accounts of the same information unless they are the "original sources" of that information. The vast majority of the federal circuits have ruled that relators' allegations are "based upon" prior public disclosures within the meaning of section 3730(e)(4) if they are "substantially similar to" or the "same as" those disclosures. It is undisputed that Wellford and Smith's allegations are the same as those previously publicly disclosed.

The Hospital contends that the District Court erred as a matter of law in denying the Hospital's motion to dismiss for lack of subject matter jurisdiction under Federal Rule of Civil Procedure 12(b)(1). The Hospital requests 30 minutes for each Party to address the issue.

JURISDICTIONAL STATEMENT

This is an appeal from an Order (not yet published) dated [Month/Day/Year] issued by the Honorable Judith Williams of the United States District Court for the District of Massachusetts. The Order denied Defendant-Appellant Hospital's Motion to Dismiss for lack of subject matter jurisdiction under Fed. R. Civ. P. 12(b)(1).

Jurisdiction in the District Court was purportedly based on 31 U.S.C. § 3730(e)(4). Jurisdiction in this Court on appeal is invoked pursuant to 28 U.S.C. § 1292(b). The District Court

---

Margin notes:

This section is permitted by the local rules in some courts.

A jurisdictional statement is standard so that the appellate court knows the appeal is properly before it.

certified that its Order involved a controlling question of law as to which there is substantial ground for difference of opinion and that an immediate appeal might materially advance the ultimate termination of the litigation. This Court on [Month/Day/Year] granted the Hospital's petition for immediate review.

STATEMENT OF THE ISSUE
PRESENTED FOR REVIEW

The False Claims Act bars qui tam actions where a relator's allegations are "based upon" allegations that were previously disclosed publicly, unless the relator qualifies as an "original source." It is undisputed that the allegations of relators Wellford and Smith are the same as allegations that were previously disclosed publicly in a newspaper by other persons. Did the District Court err as a matter of law in asserting jurisdiction over this qui tam suit?

Most apposite statute and cases:

31 U.S.C.§ 3730(e)(4) (2000).

United States ex rel. Minn. Ass'n of Nurse Anesthetists v. Allina Health Sys. Corp., 276 F.3d 1032 (8th Cir. 2002).

United States ex rel. Findley v. FPC-Boron Employees' Club, 105 F.3d 675 (D.C. Cir. 1997).

United States ex rel. Siller v. Becton Dickinson & Co., 21 F.3d 1339 (4th Cir. 1994).

United States ex rel. Precision Co. v. Koch Indus., Inc., 971 F.2d 548 (10th Cir. 1992).

There are at least three ways to structure a statement of the issue. One is to ask a single, simple question. A second is to frame a "whether" statement. The third is to ask a question after first describing the factual and legal context in two or three prefatory sentences. Clary et al., *Advocacy on Appeal* 2d. 36-37 (West 2004).

The issue in this template is a form of the third kind of structure, advocated by Bryan Garner. *See e.g.* Bryan A. Garner, *The Winning Brief* 77-79 (Oxford U. Press 1999). Note, however, that not all courts necessarily want this type of issue statement. So know your court.

Some courts require that counsel list the most apposite statutory and case authority with the statement of the issue. The

STATEMENT OF THE CASE

A. Overview

Wellford and Smith's Complaint alleges that the Hospital has submitted false bills to the government for services to Medicare patients. The Complaint alleges that the bills violate the federal False Claims Act, 31 U.S.C. § 3729 (2000).

The Hospital denies any wrongdoing. The Hospital also contends at the threshold that the Court lacks subject matter jurisdiction over the Complaint. The District Court has denied the Hospital's Motion to Dismiss under Fed. R. Civ. P. 12(b)(1), but has certified the denial for interlocutory appeal under 28 U.S.C. § 1292(b). This appeal follows this Court's grant of the Hospital's petition for immediate review.

B. Fact Statement

For purposes of this appeal, the following matters are undisputed:

Commonwealth is located in Boom Town, Massachusetts. Plaintiff's Complaint ("Pl.'s Compl.") ¶ 3 (Month Day, 20xx.), Joint Appendix ("App.") 10. The Hospital treats patients whose costs are covered by private insurance and patients whose costs are covered by Medicare. *Id.* at ¶ 4, App. 10. In the case of the latter patients, the Hospital bills the federal government according to regulations established by the federal Department of Health and Human Services. *Id.* The regulations require hospitals to bill the government only for (a) necessary services and procedures that (b) are actually provided. *Id.* at ¶ 5, App. 10. The regulations set a maximum fee for each service or medical procedure. *Id.* at ¶ 6, App. 11. The maximum fee is generally lower than what the Hospital charges its private patients for the same service or procedure. *Id.*

Unlike most hospitals, which usually rely on independent physicians, Commonwealth employs several of the surgeons who have privileges at the Hospital. *Id.* at ¶ 10, App. 12. Wellford is one such employed surgeon. *Id.* at ¶ 2, App. 10; Affidavit of Lucy Summers ("Aff. Summers") at ¶ 4, App. 20.

First Circuit does not, but you may want to put in a list anyway. If you do, confine it to the three or four most important authorities.

Many of the facts from the District Court brief may be re-used in the First Circuit brief under the circumstances. The one major difference is in citation practice. Federal appellate courts require counsel to prepare an Appendix, preferably a joint Appendix, that contains the relevant evidentiary material for convenient reference. Accordingly, cites must now include a reference to the appropriate Appendix pages. If the briefs of the parties are submitted before the relevant Appendix or Appendices are fully prepared, there are procedures for amending the

Commonwealth also employs billing personnel, one of whom is Smith. *Id.* For the last three years, Wellford and Smith have been secretly making copies at random of surgical and billing records relating to procedures performed on Medicare patients by employed surgeons at Commonwealth. Pl.'s Compl. at ¶ 13, App. 13. The copying was unauthorized and violates patient confidentiality. Aff. Summers ¶ 4, App. 20.

After examining the records, Wellford and Smith assumed that the Hospital was billing the government for procedures that were either unnecessary or never performed as reported. Pl.'s Compl. at ¶ 15, App. 14. Wellford and Smith presumed that the billing was intentional, and that the purpose and effect were to evade the fee limits and to overcharge the government. *Id.* at ¶ 16, App. 14. Wellford and Smith further presumed that the Hospital was committing fraud in violation of 31 U.S.C. § 3729, also known as the federal False Claims Act. *Id.* at ¶ 17, App. 15.

Prior to the filing of the present lawsuit, the *Boom Town Dispatch*, the local newspaper, published a lengthy article concerning the billing practices of a number of area hospitals, including Commonwealth. *Id.* at ¶ 18, App. 15; Affidavit of Sandy Andrews ("Aff. Andrews") at ¶ 3, Ex. One, App. 23. The article included a detailed discussion of Commonwealth's billing of Medicare. Aff. Andrews at ¶ 3, Ex. One, App. 23. The article quoted a number of unnamed sources as alleging that the Hospital has routinely over billed the government. *Id.* The sources claimed to identify specific examples. *Id.* The reporter who wrote the article has signed an affidavit that Wellford and Smith were *not* among the sources. Aff. Andrews at ¶ 4, App. 23. Wellford and Smith's Complaint allegations mirror the *Dispatch* article's content.

Shortly after the *Dispatch* story was published, and without having first notified the government of their information or intentions, Wellford and Smith brought an action under seal in federal district court in Boom Town. Pl.'s Compl. at ¶ 19, App. 16. They sued the Hospital under 31 U.S.C. § 3730, the qui tam provision in the False Claims Act, which allows individuals with knowledge of fraud on the government to sue on behalf of the government. *Id.* at ¶ 1, App. 9. They complied with 31

briefs to add the appropriate page references.

U.S.C. § 3730(b)(2) when filing their complaint. *Id.* at ¶ 20, App. 16. The government, pursuant to 31 U.S.C. § 3730(b)(4)(B), has declined to take over the action, leaving Wellford and Smith free to go forward as "relators."

Although the Hospital has adamantly denied any wrongdoing, and is planning a vigorous defense, its position for present purposes is simply that, taking the above information as given, the Court should dismiss the Complaint under Fed. R. Civ. P. 12(b)(1) for lack of federal subject matter jurisdiction.

SUMMARY OF THE ARGUMENT

The False Claims Act's jurisdictional bar, 31 U.S.C. § 3730(e)(4), precludes qui tam suits where a relator's allegations are "based upon" the "same" allegations that were previously publicly disclosed, unless that relator is an "original source" of the relevant information. This is the view of the vast majority of federal courts that have interpreted the Act's jurisdictional bar.

Commonwealth seeks dismissal under Fed. R. Civ. P. 12(b)(1) of the qui tam suit brought by Wellford and Smith, because Wellford and Smith cannot establish that the District Court has subject matter jurisdiction. The District Court erred in denying the dismissal for two reasons.

First, federal courts are courts of limited jurisdiction. Statutes conferring jurisdiction on federal courts are to be strictly construed. The District Court liberally construed the False Claims Act's jurisdictional bar so as to permit qui tam actions where a relator's allegations are the same as allegations that have been previously publicly disclosed, even when the relator is not an original source, so long as the relator did not "derive" his or her allegations from the public disclosure. That liberal construction flies in the face of the limited jurisdiction principle.

Second, if "based upon" means only "derived from," as the District Court ruled, then the "original source" provision is rendered impermissibly superfluous. The "derived from" construction violates the standard rule of statutory interpretation that a statute should be construed so as not to render any of its

Most appellate courts require a summary of the argument. A good rule of thumb is that an appellate court should be able to read your Statement of the Case/Facts, as well as your Summary of the Argument, and know in a nutshell (a) exactly what you want it to do, (b) why that is the right thing to do, and (c) how the court can get to the desired result.

Note that the Summary of the Argument is not the place for all of the technical citations. It is the overall road map to the argument that will follow thereafter.

terms superfluous. The District Court's construction is inconsistent with Congress' intent to preclude qui tam actions that simply repeat allegations that have already been publicly disclosed.

It is undisputed that Wellford and Smith's allegations are the same as the allegations that were previously publicly disclosed in the *Dispatch*. It is also undisputed that Wellford and Smith are not "original sources." Thus, the District Court should have dismissed Wellford and Smith's Complaint for lack of subject matter jurisdiction.

ARGUMENT

I.   AS A MATTER OF LAW, THE DISTRICT COURT ERRED IN ASSERTING SUBJECT MATTER JURISDICTION IN THE QUI TAM ACTION AGAINST COMMONWEALTH HOSPITAL.

This Court has yet to consider the parameters of the federal False Claim Act's jurisdictional bar, but most of the other circuits have addressed the issue. Although the circuit courts are split, they are not split evenly. *See United States v. LaFortune*, 192 F.3d 157, 160 (1st Cir. 1999) (noting a split among the circuits was not evenly divided and adopting the majority view). The vast majority of courts have ruled that when a relator's allegations are the same as or similar to allegations that have already been publicly disclosed, then the relator cannot demonstrate that the court has jurisdiction unless the relator qualifies as an "original source." The courts have based their rulings on the text of the statute, canons of statutory interpretation, and the legislative history.

This Court reviews the District Court's failure to dismiss for lack of subject matter jurisdiction involving a pure question of law *de novo*. *Gonzalez v. United States*, 285 F.3d 281, 287 (1st Cir. 2002).

A.   Federal Statutes Conferring Jurisdiction Are Strictly Construed.

Jurisdiction in federal court is never presumed for the

The major point heading introduces the arguments. Generally, it is directly related to the issue presented.

Provide an introduction to the issue. Identify the standard of review on appeal. This identification is an important component of a standard appellate brief. Additionally, where there is more than one argument, the introduction also signals the discrete substantive arguments that follow. Be careful not to merely repeat the Summary of the Argument.

Provide a minor point heading that relates to the

reason that federal courts have limited jurisdiction. *Viqueira v. First Bank*, 140 F.3d 12, 16 (1st Cir. 1998). If a statute confers jurisdiction on the federal courts, as does the False Claims Act, then the court must strictly construe the jurisdictional provision. *United States ex rel. Precision Co. v. Koch Indus., Inc.*, 971 F.2d 548, 552 (10th Cir. 1992). Where doubts persist, the court must rule *against* federal jurisdiction. *Id.*

Accordingly, the District Court impermissibly interpreted the jurisdictional bar of the False Claims Act as broadly conferring the court with jurisdiction anytime a relator's allegations are not "derived from" the publicly disclosed allegations.

B. The False Claims Act's Jurisdictional Bar Precludes Qui Tam Actions That Are Based on Allegations That Have Been Publicly Disclosed, Unless the Relator Qualifies as an "Original Source."

Interpreting the jurisdictional bar of the False Claims Act first requires an examination of the relevant text. *Brady v. Credit Recovery Co.*, 160 F.3d 64, 66 (1st Cir. 1998). If the proposed meaning renders the provision ambiguous, or leads to unreasonable results, then the Court must look to canons of statutory construction and the legislative history. *Id.*

The subject matter jurisdiction provision in the False Claims Act states:

> (A) *No court shall have jurisdiction* over an action under this section *based upon* the *public disclosure* of allegations or transactions . . . from the *news media, unless* the action is brought by the Attorney General or the person bringing the action is an *original source* of the information. (B) For purposes of this paragraph, 'original source' means an individual who has direct and independent knowledge of the information on which the allegations are based *and* has voluntarily *provided* the information to the Government *before filing* an action under

---

discrete argument or part of the argument you are making. Most often, it is advisable to begin with more general propositions, then move to the more specific. Note the basic IRAC structure. Here, the application and conclusion are combined.

Provide the next minor point heading, which may also serve as an introduction.

Note that this thesis paragraph accomplishes three things. First, it provides a process for the court to follow in interpreting the statute, which is consistent with the advocate's strategy. Second, it provides a subtle roadmap for the arguments that follow. Finally, it introduces the relevant rule.

this section which is based on the information.

31 U.S.C. § 3730(e)(4) (2000) (emphasis supplied).

When a defendant contests jurisdiction under this provision in a case not brought by the Attorney General, the court must make the following inquiries:

1. Has there been a public disclosure of the relevant allegations?

| Break apart the rule, providing the separate elements.

2. If yes, does the relator who brings the suit on behalf of the government base his or her claims upon the public disclosure?

3. If yes, then is the relator an "original source" of the information within the meaning of the statute?

| Note that the advocate in this appellate setting will now cite to the opinions of other circuits, rather than to a lower court opinion within the circuit.

Minn. Ass'n of Nurse Anesthetists v. Allina Health Sys. Corp., 276 F.3d 1032, 1042 (8th Cir. 2002).

Two of these elements, 1 and 3, are undisputed and indisputable in the present case: The allegations that Wellford and Smith have made against the Hospital also have been made in a newspaper report that pre-dates the filing of their Complaint. And Wellford and Smith are not "original sources" within the meaning of § 3730(e)(4)(B), because they did not provide their information to the government before they filed their Complaint. Accordingly, if the Complaint is "based upon" the newspaper article, there is no subject matter jurisdiction.

| Apply the rule to the facts and dispense with those elements that are not at issue. Focus the Court's attention on the disputed element.

The False Claims Act does not define "based upon." And a straight textual reading of the jurisdictional bar does not resolve the ambiguity. If "based upon" means merely "derived from," as the lower court ruled, then the "original source" provision is superfluous, which violates a fundamental principle of statutory construction. *See Brady*, 160 F.3d at 67 (interpreting a statutory provision and stating that one interpretation would render another provision "impermissibly superfluous") (citing *Bailey v. United States* 516 U.S. 137, 145 (1995)).

| Provide the Court with the "crux" of the problem. Set the stage for more development of the rule section—here, how other courts have interpreted the critical language. Note

1. "Based upon" means "the same as" or "substantially similar to" information or evidence that has been publicly disclosed.

The most recent circuit to interpret the jurisdictional bar of the False Claims Act ruled that a qui tam action is "based upon" a public disclosure if the relator's allegations and the publicly disclosed allegations are the same. *Minn. Ass'n of Nurse Anesthetists*, 276 F.3d at 1047. This is also the view of the vast majority of federal circuit courts. *See United States ex rel. Mistick PBT v. Hous. Auth. of Pittsburgh*, 186 F.3d 376, 386-88 (3d Cir. 1999); *United States ex rel. Biddle v. Bd. of Trustees of Leland Stanford Jr. Univ.*, 161 F.3d 533, 536-40 (9th Cir. 1998); *United States ex rel. McKenzie v. BellSouth Telecomm., Inc.*, 123 F.3d 935, 940-41 (6th Cir. 1997); *United States ex rel. Findley v. FPC-Boron Employees' Club*, 105 F.3d 675, 682-85 (D.C. Cir. 1997); *Cooper v. Blue Cross and Blue Shield of Fla., Inc.*, 19 F.3d 562, 566-67 (11th Cir. 1994); *Precision Co.*, 971 F.2d at 552-53; *United States ex rel. Doe v. John Doe Corp.*, 960 F.2d 318, 324 (2d Cir. 1992).

In *Minnesota Association of Nurse Anesthetists*, the relators brought a qui tam action against various hospitals and anesthesiologists, alleging that the defendants defrauded the government by overcharging for their services. In adopting the majority rule, the Eighth Circuit reasoned that "based upon" means the "same as" because any other construction would render the "original source" provision of the jurisdictional bar meaningless. 276 F.3d at 1047.

Similarly, in *Mistick*, the relator alleged that the defendants, a city housing authority and an architectural firm, defrauded the government by making false claims to the Department of Housing and Urban Development. In adopting the majority view, the court reasoned that an alternative construction to "based upon" would render the "original source" provision superfluous. 186 F.3d at 386.

And in . . .

. . .

---

how the advocate signals a counterargument that will be fleshed out in subsequent sections.

Develop the rule section as necessary.

Note that the advocate has often referred to the relevant section of the statute not by its numerical designation, but by its function—a jurisdictional bar, which is consistent with the advocate's overall theme.

Begin to synthesize the cases—in the present context the reasoning is more important to the advocate than a factual analysis of each case. On other occasions, the factual story in each case will be vital. For brevity, we have omitted part of the case summary in this model. However, in constructing such a summary, be careful not to merely present a case digest. Instead, weave the

The majority rule recognizes that it is impermissible to render one part of a statute superfluous when there is another construction that provides coherency and consistency and effects Congress' intent. *See United States v. Nordic Village, Inc.*, 503 U.S. 30, 36 (1992) (stating the "settled rule" is that a statute "must, if possible, be construed in such a fashion that every word has some operative effect").

2. Congress intended to limit federal qui tam actions that repeat information the government already possesses.

Congress initially enacted the qui tam provisions of the False Claims Act of 1863 to encourage private citizens to bring suit against those who defrauded the government. *Findley*, 105 F.3d at 679 (providing an in-depth discussion of the legislative history). As an inducement, the Act permitted a successful qui tam relator to collect one-half of what was recovered. *Id.*

The inducement worked. As government spending increased, especially in the 1930s and 1940s, qui tam litigation increased—"opportunistic private litigants chased after generous case bounties" by bringing parasitic lawsuits copied directly from publicly disclosed information. *Id.* at 679-80. The Act provided no effective mechanism to prevent these parasitic suits. As a result, the government gained no new information and recovered less. *Id.* at 680.

These parasitic suits reached their nadir when the Supreme Court allowed a qui tam action where the relator simply copied the allegations in his complaint directly from an indictment for criminal fraud. *Id.* (citing and discussing *United States ex rel. Marcus v. Hess*, 317 U.S. 537 (1943)). Congress reacted and amended the Act in 1943, barring "qui tam suits that were 'based upon evidence or information in the possession of the United States . . . at the time such suit was brought.' " *Id.* (quoting 57 Stat. 608). Thus, qui tam actions were barred if the evidence or information was already in possession of the government, even if the relator was the one who informed the government. *Id.*

Predictably, the pendulum swung to the other extreme.

---

analysis by staying focused on the common thread—here, that the "original source" provision has no effect if "based upon" does not mean the "same as" or "similar to." Then briefly state the pattern you have synthesized from the cases.

Where necessary, continue the rule section. Here, the legislative history provides additional support for the construction being advocated.

Note that although the advocate has chosen not to delve deeply into the legislative history, some context is important to develop the rule explanation. Here, the advocate is deliberately relying on the D.C. Circuit's discussion of the legislative history because of its depth and breadth.

In 1984, the Seventh Circuit ruled that the State of Wisconsin was precluded from proceeding in a qui tam action because the government was already in possession of the evidence. Yet it was Wisconsin that exposed the fraud and reported it to the government. *Id.* (citing and discussing *United States ex rel. Wis. v. Dean*, 729 F.2d 1100 (7th Cir. 1984). Thus, "[q]ui tam actions under the FCA had gone in forty years from unrestrained profiteering to a flaccid enforcement tool." *Doe,* 960 F.2d at 321(recounting the legislative history of the False Claims Act).

Congress reacted once again and amended the Act, precluding qui tam actions if the relator's allegations were based upon transactions or allegations that had been publicly disclosed, unless the attorney general brought the action or the relator was an "original source." *Findley,* 105 F.3d at 681.

Preventing parasitic lawsuits was not Congress' only concern.

> From its inception, the qui tam provisions of the [False Claims Act] were designed to inspire whistleblowers to come forward promptly with information concerning fraud so that the government can stop it and recover ill-gotten gains. Once the information is in the public domain, there is less need for a financial incentive to spur individuals into exposing frauds. Allowing qui tam suits after that point may either pressure the government to prosecute cases when it has good reasons not to or reduce the government's ultimate recovery.

Id. at 686. *See also Biddle*, 161 F.3d at 538-39.

Indeed, nowhere in the legislative history is there evidence that Congress intended "based upon" to mean something other than repeating, or "parroting," information already available to the government. *See Findley,* 105 F.3d at 684-85. Where a relator's allegations merely repeat publicly disclosed information, and the relator does not qualify as an "original source," the court lacks jurisdiction.

As a general rule, long quotes from opinions are not helpful. But here, the advocate chose to rely on the court's language to impress upon the instant court that Congress intended more than just preventing parasitic lawsuits.

Conclude the rule section with a description of what the rule means.

In the instant case, it is undisputed that the *Dispatch* published an article concerning the billing practices of various area hospitals, including Commonwealth. Pl.'s Compl. at ¶ 18, App. 15; Aff. Andrews ¶ 3, Ex. One, App. 23. It is undisputed that the article was published before Wellford and Smith brought this qui tam action. *Id.* And it is undisputed that the article included a detailed discussion of Commonwealth's billing of Medicare. Aff. Andrews ¶ 3, Ex. One, App. 23. The article identified specific alleged examples of fraudulent billing practices. *Id.* A simple facial comparison of Wellford and Smith's Complaint with the article reveals that the allegations mirror each other. Thus, by definition, the allegations in the Complaint are the same as or similar to the publicly disclosed allegations in the newspaper article. This similarity means, as a matter of law, that the lower court lacked subject matter jurisdiction in this case, as Wellford and Smith are not proper plaintiffs under the False Claims Act. To decide otherwise, as the lower court did, impermissibly renders the "original source" provision meaningless and fails to effect Congress' intent in enacting the jurisdictional bar to the False Claims Act.

> Apply the reasoning to the instant facts.

> Provide, if helpful, a brief conclusion.

C. The District Court Erred in Relying on *Siller* and Asserting Jurisdiction Over This Qui Tam Action.

One circuit has advanced the minority view of what "based upon" means. In *United States ex rel. Siller v. Becton Dickinson & Co.*, 21 F.3d 1339 (4th Cir. 1994), the court ruled that "based upon" means "derived from." The court further explained that a "relator's action is 'based upon' a public disclosure of allegations only where the relator has actually derived from that disclosure the allegations upon which his qui tam action is based." *Id.* at 1348.

Every other circuit to consider the meaning of "based upon" has explicitly or implicitly rejected the *Siller* court's interpretation because it violates the canons of statutory construction and fails to effect Congress' intent. (One panel of the Seventh Circuit adopted the *Siller* court's interpretation; but another panel almost simultaneously concluded that, when the allegations of a relator have been previously publicly disclosed, then the court has jurisdiction "only if" the relator is an "original

> This minor point heading introduces the key counterargument and refutation. In the trial brief, the advocate chose to weave the counterargument addressing the adverse authority within the rule section. Here, the advocate provides a discrete argument that follows the IRAC formula.

source" of the facts. *Compare United States v. Bank of Farmington*, 166 F.3d 853, 863 (7th Cir. 1999*) with United States ex rel. Lamers, v. City of Green Bay*, 168 F.3d 1013, 1017 (7th Cir. 1999)).

The *Siller* court relied principally on an isolated textual reading of the "based upon" clause. In doing so, it created a construction that is inconsistent with the federal courts' limited jurisdiction; is inconsistent with the "original source" provision; and is inconsistent with Congress' intent to preclude relator standing for would-be plaintiffs who parrot information the government already has.

In relying on *Siller*, the District Court similarly violated canons of statutory interpretation, adopting a construction that leads to unreasonable results.

The District Court's reliance on two prior decisions within the District was also misplaced. In *United States ex rel. LaValley v. First National Bank of Boston*, 707 F. Supp. 1351, 1367 (D. Mass. 1988), the court first had to decide whether the 1986 False Claims Act amendments that resulted in 31 U.S.C. § 3730(e)(4)(A) and (B) should even apply retroactively to a case filed in 1985. The vast majority of the court's opinion was devoted to that question. When the court did reach the "based upon" definitional issue, it did so without the benefit of any of the later circuit court precedent.

Similarly, in *United States ex rel. LeBlanc v. Raytheon Co.*, 874 F. Supp. 35, 41 (D. Mass. 1995), *aff'd*, 62 F.3d 1411 (1st Cir. 1995), the court stated that it did not matter whether the plaintiff's allegations were derived from or merely similar to the prior public disclosures in the case, because LeBlanc failed to establish subject matter jurisdiction under either test. Thus, the court's preference for one definition over the other was dictum. And, because the First Circuit's affirmance was an unpublished, summary one, the fact of the affirmance is of no precedential value in the present case. *See* 1st Cir. R. 36(c), 32.3.

The District Court should have followed the reasoning of the court in *United States ex rel. O'Keeffe v. Sverdup Corp.*, 131 F. Supp. 2d 87 (D. Mass. 2001). In that case, the plaintiff

The advocate chose to briefly, but strongly, summarize the weaknesses in the adverse authority rather than synthesize the reasoning of the other cases rejecting this interpretation. Either strategy, depending upon the circumstances, may be effective.

Here, the advocate must also address the split among the judges within the District.

alleged that the defendants had falsified the results of an engineering study of the environmental impact of the proposed restoration of commuter rail service in Southeastern Massachusetts. Because both the allegedly false facts and the allegedly true facts were publicly disclosed in the documents and hearings relating to the rail project, the court ruled that the complaint was "based upon" the prior public disclosures, and granted summary judgment for the defense when plaintiff could not establish that he was an original source of the relevant information. *Id.* at 100.

The *O'Keeffe* court reviewed the split among the federal circuits, adopted the majority view, and explicitly rejected the reasoning of *LeBlanc* and *LaValley*. *Id.* at 92-93. The court correctly summarized the two primary reasons why "based upon" means "similar to or the same." First, Congress amended the public disclosure jurisdictional bar in 1986 as part of a complex balancing of competing public interests. On the one hand, Congress wanted to provide inside whistleblowers with incentives to come forward with valuable information concerning fraud upon the government. On the other hand, Congress sought to discourage suits based upon information already in the possession of federal authorities. *Id.* at 91 (citing *United States ex rel. Springfield Terminal Ry. Co. v. Quinn*, 14 F.3d 645, 649 (D.C. Cir. 1994)).

Second, if "based upon" means only "derived from," then the "original source" requirement is rendered superfluous. By definition, if a relator's allegations are not derived from prior public disclosures, the relator has direct and independent knowledge of his claims. *Id.* at 93. The fact that Congress thought it necessary to write an original source exception into § 3730(e)(4) must mean that Congress intended a broader view of the term "based upon" than simply "derived from." *Id.*

CONCLUSION

[For all of the above reasons, the Court should reverse the ruling of the District Court and dismiss the Complaint for lack of subject matter jurisdiction.]

[This Court should reverse the ruling of the District

Two types of conclusion are possible. One is an abbreviated form, that can be desirable to avoid repetition in an otherwise short brief. The other is a longer, more

Court and dismiss the Complaint for lack of subject matter jurisdiction. The relators have based their Complaint upon publicly disclosed allegations. The Complaint is merely parasitical in that it is based upon information the Government already has. 31 U.S.C. § 3730(e)(4) bars the Complaint.]

Dated: April 1, 2003

Respectfully submitted,

Eve Johnson, #87623
Matters & Johnson
25 Winner Way
Boom Town, MA 01000
(617) 765-4321

Eve Johnson

Attorney for Appellant
Commonwealth Hospital, Inc.

descriptive form that can be a useful bookend to the initial Summary of the Argument in an otherwise long brief. Reasonable lawyers may disagree over which form of conclusion to use. Part of the answer depends upon your audience. If you know that the relevant judge or judges like to jump to the end of a brief for the punch line before they read the full brief, you may want to opt for the longer, more descriptive form.

Note: Make sure that you present your relevant identifying information, date the brief, and sign it.

CERTIFICATE OF COMPLIANCE
[as to the length of the brief]

ADDENDUM
[containing relevant district court opinion
and any other material required]

Attach these items
to the brief.

QUICK REFERENCE INDEX
To Lists, Tables, and Templates

Analysis
    Good features of, vi
    Presentation levels of, 150
    Six key principles of, iii

Authority/Rules
    Assembling a rule templates
        from a case, 44
        from multiple cases, 53
        in direct conflicts, 65
        in issue of first impression, 69
        from a statute, 79
    Basic principles, 25
    Common mistakes
        in assembling a rule, 61
        in parsing a rule, 36
    Identifying sources, 30
    Sources of, 19
    Working with cases chart, 29
    Working with statutes chart, 29

Citations
    ALWD Citation Manual, 107
    The Bluebook, 122
    When and What to Cite, 141

Document Templates
    Appellate Brief, 205
    Client Letter, 162
    Office Memorandum, 155
    Pre-trial Motion papers, 183

Organization
    Basic IRAC components, 86
    Linking IRACs outline, 94
    Linking IRACs example, 95
    Road Mapping table, 8

Writing
    Common mistakes to avoid, 103
    Good features of, vi
    Persuasive, features of, 170
    Predictive, features of, 146
    Six key principles, iii

Add your own quick references: